MIZLANSKY/ ZILINSKY

OR

"Schmucks"

MIZLANSKY/ ZILINSKY

OR

"Schmucks"

JON ROBIN BAITZ

THEATRE COMMUNICATIONS GROUP

This publication is made possible in part with public funds from the New York State Council on the Arts, a State Agency.

"Playwright's Collaborator: The Kid He Used to Be," by Jon Robin Baitz, was previously published in the February 1, 1998 edition of the *New York Times,* and is copyright © 1998 by the New York Times Company. Reprinted by permission.

Baitz, Jon Robin, 1961–
Mizlansky/Zilinsky or "Schmucks" / Jon Robin Baitz.—1st ed.
p. cm.
ISBN 1-55936-160-3 (pbk. : alk. paper)
1. Motion picture producers and directors—California—Los Angeles—Drama.
I. Title.
PS3552.A393 M59   1998
812'.54—dc21
98–49476
CIP

Cover art and design by Spot Design
Text design and composition by Lisa Govan

First Edition, December 1998

For the original New York cast—Jennifer Albano, Mark Blum, Glenn Fitzgerald, Julie Kavner, Nathan Lane, Larry Pine, Paul Sand, Lewis J. Stadlen and Lee Wilkoff—an ensemble, who reminded me why I love actors so much. And for Joe, who makes my chaos look like order, both on stage and off.

J.R.B.

PLAYWRIGHT'S COLLABORATOR: THE KID HE USED TO BE

JON ROBIN BAITZ

LIKE MANY WRITERS, I have a drawer dedicated to abandoned and unmanageable projects, notes on unlikely subjects, faux aphorisms and fake profundity. My "drawer of misery" is full of false starts, wonderful little trinkets of flash and mortification.

By far, the longest tenant of this drawer is a slim, one-act piece of playwriting from 1984 called *Mizlansky/Zilinsky,* about the lives of some desperate cases on the fringes of the movie world. It was my first produced work, presented at a minuscule theatre (now a 1950s furniture store, of course), just off Melrose Avenue in Los Angeles, on a couple of Monday, Tuesday and Wednesday nights for one month in 1985, when someone else's show was dark (a play by the vastly underappreciated California playwright John Steppling).

For a while, in the late 1980s, I intended to return to it, but gradually, as the drawer became fuller, and other subjects became more pressing, I moved on.

I had not thought of *M/Z* for years, when, last summer, L.A. Theater Works (the original producers) asked for permission to revive the play for radio. I consented, under the misapprehension that it meant no real work for me. Then, a month before they were to record it, I looked at the pages for the first time in eight years and realized that there was trouble: what I found was the unformed writing of a young man, oblique strands of narrative and some funny and perhaps useful exchanges.

The thought of its being recorded was unbearable. I went

back to work on the piece out of shame and fear (those twin slave drivers). But now, I was thirty-six years old, and no longer so facile. And, I was still recovering from the mortality shock of having undergone sudden open-heart surgery. The year had left me more fragile than I realized, with perhaps a diminished capacity for laughter, boldness or bravery. This is not a useful state for writing, so I jumped at the opportunity to open my drawer of misery and possibly let some light back into my life.

In so doing, I found I was collaborating with a more exuberant, more encouraging version of myself. Unsettling and reviving all at once, it felt as though I were administering a kind of literary CPR on myself.

The world of the play came back vividly: the old pages hinted at a darker California, which I had perhaps been too close to before, but which now offered the outline for a new work. I began the rewrite under the spell of a surprising nostalgia for the fading Los Angeles of my parents' generation (the 1950s): the Brown Derby (long gone except in ironic shadow at Disney/MGM Studios near Orlando, Florida); Cobb salads; family picnics at vast, empty, panoramic Santa Monica beaches in late summer; an oddball idiosyncratic L.A. of little villages strung together, which seemed to have disappeared (a bit like the old 42nd Street) around the time the play takes place.

I was in my early twenties and still living in L.A. in the early 1980s—the decade of big money flowing to and fro hypnotically. I had prematurely stalled out under the smog burn instead of sensibly going East to college (the first escape clause in the lifetime contracts of many native-born Californians). Though uncomfortably an Angeleno, I stayed on, and fell in with what might be labeled a "den of thieves."

My employer, whom I adored, was a middle-aged "film producer," who had stumbled out of the movie world and into a lucrative side business—selling questionable tax shelters. I picked up his laundry (were there stains remaining, I was blamed), Chinese food (the real cause of same), answered phones (danger, creditors) and fell pretty much in love with him, his pals and their vertiginously ambivalent little world.

The details of his business were so fabulously intricate, so Mandarin and elusive, that I suspect the success of the tax shelter venture lay in the artifice of its mirrorlike surface, which was impervious to the rigors of interpretation. Eventually, however, as the atmosphere of toxicity in his ambit became unbearable, I untethered myself. (Actually, I was fired in the lobby of a Washington hotel, where my employer was trying to stave off government agents who were closing in.) We saw each other only a few more times before he died, after he moved to France, in flight from the carnivorous pack of litigants snapping at his heels.

The notes I kept during that time formed the earlier play. Looking back, thirteen years later, I recalled writing under the thrall of the cool jazz riffs of improvisatory scheming (so palpable in the Watergate tapes). Jettisoning much of the old writing, I was eager to preserve and expand on that music. It held me in its spell again, especially since many more hours of Oval Office high jinks had come gloriously to light in the intervening years.

Nixon and Mizlansky shared something old-fashioned and "West Coast"—a particular verbal casualness, not to mention a vivid paranoia and a great appetite for power (though Mizlansky was as indifferent to politics as Nixon was to movie making; Mizlansky merely liked the casual, Lacoste shirt, clubhouse atmosphere of Southern California, wherein circus behavior was encouraged). Like Nixon's world, that of Mizlansky/Zilinsky and company was one of a gang of men who had a secret language all their own, and were living precariously from deal to deal as though they were in transit lounges on an endless bad flight; theirs was an existence by damage control, wherein each day ended with a sigh of relief at having made it through twenty-four hours in Coldwater Canyon without being shut down.

As the great hallucinatory L.A. sunsets closed-out businesses, there were sighs of relief and frozen margaritas. There were enemy lists, last-minute side deals and desperate attempts to make at least three last killings before some sword of Damocles came slicing down to smite them. It was all singularly male, leavened by a slight sense of also being a put-on. To my gang of outsiders, there was nothing that wasn't at least slightly comedy. Even their own rise and fall and fall . . .

At the La Brea Tar Pits, there is a marvelous, full-scale, fake mastodon, doomed and struggling. (There is an extraordinary painting of this animal at night by Robert Yarber. The mastodon seems to be fading in a night-noir fog.) The creature was much on my mind as I went back to work. He is the perfect symbol of the old L.A. of Mizlansky and Zilinsky—an old-world order of small-timers and low-key hustlers disappearing under the murk, occluded in the shadow of such 1980s titans as Boesky, Milken, Keating, et al.

Sadly, my gang was no match for the bone-deep, gimlet-eyed megasalesmanship of the new global Disney, or even the Pacific Rim cool of a Mike Ovitz. (At times, M/Z and Nixon, Inc., seem slightly innocent by comparison.) It occurred to me that the world of these men—my gang—was true and mine, and worth writing about—now, especially after a death scare and a visit from its shadow buddy, melancholia.

I sometimes think I started writing too early to know how fragile a thing it is. I spent my twenties and early thirties taking the writing life (or perhaps just life) for granted. I used to wonder why I occasionally saw such fear in the faces of some older writers, etched in under the surface. Now I think I know why: if you're listening to the wrong music, what you hear is no tune at all, except the ticking of your own ghastly big clock, not the music of the world around you.

In opening my drawer of misery, I met a new kid playwright. He didn't know much about the theatre, but he had a keen eye and a good ear, was more generous than his older counterpart, and was blessed with an easy sense of humor. I believe he helped me relocate some of those now faded qualities, as well as being a trajectory back to the world of the living—after finding myself, to paraphrase Dante, "astray in a dark wood in the middle of the journey of my life" as a writer.

JON ROBIN BAITZ
February 1, 1998
From the *New York Times*

MIZLANSKY/
ZILINSKY

OR

"Schmucks"

PRODUCTION HISTORY

The one-act *Mizlansky/Zilinsky* was produced in January 1985 by L.A. Theatre Works, Susan Albert Loewenberg, Producing Director. The full-length *Mizlansky/Zilinsky or "Schmucks"* was produced in January 1998 by Manhattan Theatre Club, Lynne Meadow, Artistic Director; Barry Grove, Executive Producer. The set was designed by Santo Loquasto, costumes by Ann Roth, lighing by Brian MacDevitt and sound design and original music composition was by David Van Tieghem. Joe Mantello directed the following cast:

PAUL TRECKER	Glenn Fitzgerald
LIONEL HART	Paul Sand
ALAN TOLKIN	Mark Blum
DUSTY FINK	Jennifer Albano
DAVIS MIZLANSKY	Nathan Lane
MILES BROOK	Lee Wilkof
SAM ZILINSKY	Lewis J. Stadlen
HORTON DE VRIES	Larry Pine

Over Speakerphone:

SYLVIA ZILINSKY	Christine Baranski
ESTHER ARTHUR	Julie Kavner
MR. BRAITHWAIT	Harry Shearer

CHARACTERS

PAUL TRECKER	Twenty-seven. Mizlansky's slave.
LIONEL HART	In his fifties. A TV actor, struggling to keep his head above water. Sweet.
ALAN TOLKIN	In his early fifties. A film producer, struggling to keep afloat. A kind man, decent.
DUSTY FINK	A masseuse.
DAVIS MIZLANSKY	In his early fifties. A film producer, tax-shelter promoter, movie-world hustler, ambivalent about it all.
MILES BROOK	Late thirties. A lawyer. Trying to hold on.
SAM ZILINSKY	Davis Mizlansky's partner, fifty-five, his best friend, also a producer. Might or might not have gone to Yale.
HORTON DE VRIES	Fifty. Out of Arkansas.

Over Speakerphone:

HOTEL RECEPTIONIST	At Casa de la Ventana del Sol.
SYLVIA ZILINSKY	Sam Zilinsky's estranged wife.
ESTHER ARTHUR	Mizlansky's second ex-wife.
MR. BRAITHWAIT	A client.

TIME AND PLACE

December 1984 and January 1985 in Los Angeles.

Prologue

Trecker appears in a tight spotlight on an otherwise entirely dark stage.

TRECKER: . . . In the beginning God created the heavens and the earth. *(Beat)* But the earth was formless and empty and darkness covered everything. And nothing happened and it seemed boring. *(Beat)* And . . . so he made mankind. (And some girls.) But mankind had no place to go. And it was cold, dark, buggy and humid. So he created a marvelous Eden on the Pacific and said: "Let there be light." And there was light.

Act One

MIZLANSKY

SCENE 1

December 14, 12:30 P.M. Lights up on Le Creche de Oaxaca, a Franco-Spanish bistro in Playa Del Rey. Tolkin and Hart at lunch.

HART: —I'm scared, Alan. You know, I'm in a thing, where, frankly, I'm on a respirator.

TOLKIN: It'll be fine, Lionel, you'll get something.

HART: I was going to play James Coburn's assistant in this thing shooting in Baja, like some Agatha Christie novella. They wrote me out. Or hired a real Mexican.

TOLKIN: It's hard for all of us now. It's a drought. Nineteen eighty-four is a drought year . . . Maybe next year will be different. I think El Niño drove people nutsy.

HART: I'm scared to get up in the morning. I can't get a job! I had my own series, for God's sake. I was *Tintoretto, Art Detective,* for three seasons and—

TOLKIN: Stop picking at that tortilla. You're making me crazy.

HART: What are those green slivers in it? They scare me!

TOLKIN: Cilantro and anchovies in a chive thing. It's baked into the corn. It's very—I don't know—it's not—I had that in Cabo. I love—don't pick at it! Eat it or don't!

HART: You *like* this? It tastes like a fish slept under it.

TOLKIN: Yeah. It has a spicy undertaste—I don't like the lemon-chili—it's not Thai but *Oaxacan*—never *mind* the food—I ran into Mizlansky—from Mizlansky/Zilinsky.

HART: Oi. He—scary—did you—are you—the mole butter, did you use it all . . . ?

TOLKIN: Mizlans—I ran into him at 9255 Sunset. I'm having the meeting with that Swedish agent, the very striking-looking

9

Nordic Jewish fellow with the blond—I mean—how is a—
I can't believe his name is Goldenberg, and he looks like
Leni Riefenstahl's nephew but with a big *mezuzah* on the
door—anyway—I run into Mizlansky in the service elevator and the man is carrying an Oak Knoll desk. It must—
it weighs six hundred pounds. And he's so nice to me, you
know, it's crazy how nice he is. Like he cared and everything!

HART *(Distracted)*: Look at that guy. He knows I need to use the
pay phone! It's so hostile!

TOLKIN: Can I finish my—I'm telling a story—Mizlansky offers
me the desk! In the elevator! Selling me a desk! Because
he says he's working out of his house from now on. He's—

HART: Working out of the house is a nice way of saying "broke."

TOLKIN: He said he's—no—he's so *"excited"*—no more movie
stuff—no more *producing*—he's into some sort of crazy tax
shelters—

HART: Tax shelters. Legal? *Legal* ones? Legal tax shelters? What?

TOLKIN: I don't know. Who knows, if it's Mizlansky. Apparently
it's—the thing is—children's Bible-story records. The master recording. *Revelation Revealed, Tales of Ancient Mesopo-
tamia, Sodom and Gomorrah: The True Story!* You know, I—he
showed me—they're on the shelf at poor people's retail
outfits—

HART: He's doing a sales pitch in the service elevator of 9255
Sunset? Be cautious!

TOLKIN: No. Listen. It's interesting. Rich midwestern rural people. Like dentists, or, I don't know, osteopaths who need a
tax shelter. Mizlansky does these Bible-story records, for
very little money. You get a huge write-off. I mean, it's a
whole business thing. It's like this: It should look like it
could *make* money. But at the end of the day, all it *does* is
lose money.

HART: Oi. It sounds like my career. Maybe they should invest in
me. Listen—did you mention our project? Is he interested
in our picture?

TOLKIN: I don't think, somehow, that a serious drama about

hidden Nazis in America is exactly what Mizlansky/Zilinsky are looking for.

HART: I always liked Zilinsky. He was classy. He used to be an agent—in fact, he was *my* agent—for two months in 1968.

TOLKIN: Mizlansky actually had—he's got a kind of charming nastiness about him. But . . . they had fun, you know? I mean the movies they made! *LSD Mamma Detective?* Remember that? So much fun!

HART *(Laughing)*: Oh God. *(Beat)* This town. From '67 to '75. It was heaven.

TOLKIN: He asked me to come over later. I think he wants to do something.

HART: You're not.

TOLKIN: No. But the thing is, it's so dangerous; you could wake up rich.

HART: I forbid it. I expressly—

TOLKIN: I don't want dessert, do you?

HART *(Wistful)*: A cookie would be nice.

TOLKIN: So we'll stop at Save-On.

HART: Alan. Don't get in with that crowd. They're not—maybe they're fun—but—they'll swallow you with a glass of water.

TOLKIN *(Looking at the menu)*: Okay. You had the Taiwan Taquitos, and I had the Chopped Chinese Chicken Tostada and the—so you owe . . . did you have two Perriers? You owe eighteen and a quarter without the—

HART *(Cutting him off)*: Why do you always do this? What—what is it with you always doing an audit at the end of lunch instead of just splitting—splitting—like regular—

TOLKIN: Because it's—you know what? It's fine, whatever you want, but I just like to be on top of things for the sake of—

HART *(Whispering)*: Well let's just split it down the middle! I'm tired of doing long division at the end of lunch all the time!

TOLKIN: Okay. So we split it.

HART *(Pointing to a girl entering the restaurant)*: Look over there. That girl! She was caught giving full-release massages in a green Citroen behind the Friar's Club last May and the

Beverly Hills police banned her from working within city limits. Then Brentwood got her. She's moving toward the beach like a virus!

TOLKIN: Poor thing. She's ended up in the marina. She can't get much further west than this.

HART *(A harsh and panicked whisper)*: Stop staring! She'll see you, you've got tortilla flecks on your chin, she can see you staring! Oh God, she's so desperate it's pathetic.

DUSTY: Lionel?

HART *(Loudly calling out)*: Hi, Dusty! My God, you look *amazing*!

(Blackout.)

SCENE 2

3:45 P.M. The same day. Lights up on Mizlansky's house in Coldwater Canyon. A fifties' ranch house with a pool. It needs some attention. Renovation work has been halfhearted. Somewhere on stage is a stationary bicycle. Mizlansky and Brook, mid-discussion. Mizlansky is barefoot and rubs his feet.

MIZLANSKY: Oh God, my feet! They swell up! From walking uphill in smog! I can't walk! The allergens! Jesus, it's like some sort of chemical weapon, you can see the spores floating up Coldwater Canyon! It's like ragweed flyin' up the canyon . . .

BROOK: You've had a lot of trouble with that car—the paint—the smell—

MIZLANSKY: It just dies halfway up the canyon! Again! I'm in this expiring Mercedes which is slipping backward toward the Beverly Hills Hotel, and nothing in it works! It's like a little German clown car! And it's making a noise like someone's grinding bratwurst in the glove compartment. I had to walk—it's just *sitting* there—

BROOK: But. I just—a little thing: can we go back to the subject? You're telling me that the IRS has called *three times* today—you're saying they've been—

MIZLANSKY: Can you not *panic*, please, it's so vulgar to see you with your eyes popping like Bela Lugosi. You know? And—your face gets distended like a silent movie. The IRS. Yes. They're sniffing. And I think the truth is Sam is having a nervous breakdown.

BROOK: Has Sam talked to the IRS? Has he blabbed?

MIZLANSKY: Not that I know of. He's not a blabby sort of guy.

BROOK: Well—is it because of the bookkeeping on the Deadly Kennel pictures? Is it *Lover of Mink? Hitler's Niece?* Because we settled—those claims were *settled* before I became your lawyer. I'm not retroactively respon—

MIZLANSKY *(Cutting him off)*: Miles. You have to—relax and smile and get used to this stuff. Don't stand there inter-rogating me, call them up, call them back, call the IRS guy and make a deal and get rid of him. Offer him something.

BROOK: What deal? *What* "get rid of him"? They—we don't even know what they *want*? I've only been your lawyer for a *year*, I don't know what you had going on—Davis, please—

MIZLANSKY *(Calm)*: Miles, this is the tax-shelter business, of course we're going to attract attention from the IRS. Just call and stall, stop waiting to stall them; stall them *now!* You can never stall too soon.

BROOK: But if Sam Zilinsky is telling them one thing and—we have to coordinate our stories—how can you have a partner in New York who's having a breakdown and try and—

MIZLANSKY: I'm doing what I can! The truth's, I can't find him. Nobody knows where he is!

BROOK: Oh my God, nobody knows where he is?

MIZLANSKY: Just sit tight; he'll turn up. He's probably hiding for a day or so. *(Beat)* You want a tangelo juice? They were at Trader Joe's, they're shipped in from this place called Isla Del Sal, which means Island of Salt. *(A magical reverie)* I wish I could buy Trader Joe's . . . sit there, stocking the shelves with nice little nuts and berries and the customers ask questions . . . and you actually *know* the answers . . .

TRECKER *(Entering with a Western Union telegram)*: I talked to the car guy—it was Achmed again—he's going to put you at the top of the list—said they'd be at the car in either ninety minutes or one hundred and twenty minutes. They'll call.

MIZLANSKY *(Horrified)*: I'm without a vehicle! This is completely unacceptable!

TRECKER *(Patient, as to a child)*: Well, I think he was very accommodating. Achmed put you first in line for service, that's all he can do, Davis. There's nothing before first.

MIZLANSKY *(Indicating the telegram)*: What have you got there?

TRECKER: A telegram from Sam. And the man who was coming to teach you how to use the pizza oven apparently died in an explosion, but his nephew will be here next Thursday. And the massage girl, Dusty, she canceled.

MIZLANSKY: Hey. Paul. A: never be accepting documents without checking first. Especially now. Okay? Now is not the time to be cleverly signing for things without first knowing what you're signing for. Also, B: don't answer the phone— let the service pick up—

TRECKER *(Whining)*: It's just a telegram from Sam, it's not like it's a subpoena.

MIZLANSKY: Don't even joke. Don't play a game with me. Okay. Hey. Now, Paul: did you get to Esther's? Did you get the thing I told you to get?

TRECKER *(Defensive)*: I got the thing. It was like fine. I got it.

MIZLANSKY: And nobody saw you *take* the thing?

TRECKER: I got the thing and I dropped it off at Peretzian Gallery on Melrose like you said to! God, I know how to do . . . things.

BROOK *(Alert)*: What thing?

MIZLANSKY: Nothing. Paul. Did you finish writing the *Book of Job*?

TRECKER: I'm still working on it—it's a lot of—the—it's depressing—I can't get Satan's voice quite right—

MIZLANSKY: How long does it take to do some plagues? It's just—the whole thing is about boils. Come on. Don't be a kid. Be a good grown-up. Do your job and finish Job. If you need help, I'll rewrite it. Believe me, I know that story.

TRECKER *(Whining)*: Well it's just that you keep giving me other stuff to do and I—you know—

MIZLANSKY *(Disgust and disdain)*: *I'll* finish it, you go to Gelson's and get a couple of tins of Italian tuna. Not the Portuguese. The Italian with the caper on the tin. The caper and the flower. *(Beat)* That's actually a good porn title.

TRECKER *(Snickering)*: Also, you have a Cairo-podist appointment—you're late for the allergist and the shoemaker—

MIZLANSKY *(Furious)*: "*Cairo*—podist"? Hey! Just go and don't tell me in that tone of snideness where I have to be, I know where I have to be and you're lucky you have somewhere to be too! Now go for the tuna!—an even better porn title!—and another thing: are you sure you didn't steal those ancient Egyptian ceramic cats I have?

TRECKER: You think I stole a pair of ceramic cats? Is that what this is?

MIZLANSKY: Did you? Because I was just offered cash for the pair—eighty-two thousand in cash—give 'em back and we can split—tell me—*amnesty*—did you take them? I need both of them for this deal. You took them, right? I understand if you did—a weak moment—I do stuff like that all the time, I ran into the Beverly Hills Cheese Shop once and stole a hunk of Emmenthaler—

TRECKER *(Defensive)*: No! God! I did not steal your cats! Get off my head! Man! You know, I'm not your butler! You hired me to be a story editor, and I'm just like—*laundry* boy!

(Trecker exits.)

MIZLANSKY *(Sighs)*: He's such a smart-ass little spoilt Beverly Hills snot. I found him and saved him from the *depths* of his laziness, and all he does all day long is betray me nonstop like it's a *spectator sport*.

(He crosses to a small exercise bike.)

Read—read Sam's telegram—

BROOK *(Reading the note)*: "Davis. I've made costly decisions all
my life. Stop. Now the IRS came to the office and I stood
high above Sixth Avenue and wanted to jump from the
Mies van der Rohe black slate and into the black Manhattan night. Stop."

MIZLANSKY: Stop! He's a terrible writer with awful pretensions.

BROOK *(Reading on)*: "The IRS is after us because of you and
your lies and me and my weakness and today as I tottered
on the brink of the end, I tabbed the losses that have
brought me to my knees. My wife, my children—"

MIZLANSKY: His children? Chronic underachievers with the
complexions of nonstop masturbators, all of them—
furtive *sweaty kids*—and the boy? His breath! Like, I swear
to God, a cheese shop in hell!

BROOK: Can I finish reading, please, Davis? "Today I did something I should have done years ago: I stole the money . . .
(Reading with increasing dismay) you *deposited in the Cayman
Islands. (Pause)* All four *hundred thousand.* That you have
appropriated from others and laundered."

(Pause.)

MIZLANSKY: That money was my emergency! Christ!

BROOK: Davis! You hid money?

MIZLANSKY: In case of trouble. It was good for a little life raft.

BROOK: Oh God, Oh God, Davis: I'm not supposed to know
these things! I am an officer of the court! *(Beat)* Maybe we
should think about pulling the plug . . . ?

MIZLANSKY: We can't. You know, I can't even afford to have my
big Christmas party this year; there's no money for it. You
were here last year; the place lights up, people laughing,
damn it.

BROOK: Davis. I'm sorry.

MIZLANSKY: It's not even a *real* nervous breakdown: it's a *walking* kind, like a twenty-four-hour bug, you can still smile and sign papers and go to lunch.

BROOK: But is he competent?

MIZLANSKY: Insomuch as he's utterly insane, sure. Move, will you, you're sitting at an angle right in front of the sun and you keep leaning so it's like a *jabbing* in my eyes—

BROOK *(Reading)*: "Firnbach from the IRS has a file on us. He had that dangerous fat-boy gleam in his eyes that they get when they go after a fellow Jew. He will never quit."

MIZLANSKY: What hurts me is to see a nice person who had the raw potential to run this town be reduced to this kind of undignified vulgarity and paranoia on the basis of one little *nudge* from the IRS.

BROOK *(Going on)*: "The Cayman money I see as legitimately mine as you have ruined any future earning potential I might have had. I will be in L.A. tonight. Staying at the Casa de la Ventana del Sol on Wilshire in Westwood. We will talk. Sam."

MIZLANSKY *(Moaning)*: Not good. Not good. Not good.

BROOK: What if the IRS tracked the Cayman money?

MIZLANSKY: I was very careful. I know how to hide money. Believe me, I grew up hiding money, I know how to hide money offshore. I could hide money from myself and never find it; in fact, I have.

BROOK: I need to know what you've done that could leave us exposed!

MIZLANSKY *(Casual)*: Well. Last year, when we started the Bible-story thing, I kept selling shelters past December thirty-first and then backdated the papers. I'm sorry I never told you, but I didn't think it was a big deal.

BROOK: So you committed *fraud*? That's what they have, is it, Davis? Backdating papers?

MIZLANSKY: The phones were ringing, and the buyers were clamoring, and I was *selling*. It was *harmless*, it was a *service* to the busy client who couldn't close before the end of the year, and ultimately who cares?

BROOK *(Hysterical)*: The IRS! The IRS is not so sympathetic to cavalier, capricious attitudes to *dates!* Davis. *Dates* are all they have! They put people in jail. They send you to white-collar prisons where politicians write books and are born again and rape you!

(Pause.)

MIZLANSKY: Hey. Look. Sweetness. Miles. My friend. You must think money is some sort of easy thing. Two years ago I was utterly in debt, living in a two-bedroom apartment near Ships coffee shop, off La Cienega. I did not pull myself out of the south side of Chicago to end up staring at a toaster at Ships, waiting for raisin toast to pop up. When we came up with this scheme, I realized I was on the verge of being able to protect my family, my ex-wives, my friends. Now here we are, we have one big deal to close, the accountant from Enid, Oklahoma, Horton De Vries. *(Beat)* You get us through this time and you walk away with two percent of that deal. Two percent of ten million. From that deal alone.

Just fight the IRS guy, hand to hand if you have to, from room to room, like a *mensch*. And I have to tell you now how much I love you, how much I respect and adore and am jealous of your talent and your brain, your whole *look*, the way you manage to—and if you play it right, you'll run this town.

BROOK *(After a choked-up moment of silent embarrassment)*: Maybe you should call Sam at the Casa de la Ventana del Sol? See if he'll soften.

(Mizlansky looks through a massive Rolodex on his desk. Then punches the numbers into the phone.)

MIZLANSKY *(To Brook)*: I gotta close these deals, Miles. I've got construction people, I bought a little Hockney at that UJA auction—it's not the first time—we had a big incident in Spain once—on the set of *Bugzilla*—

HOTEL RECEPTIONIST *(Over speakerphone)*: Casa de la Ventana del Sol.

MIZLANSKY *(To the voice)*: Hello? Sam Zilinsky please.

HOTEL RECEPTIONIST *(Over speakerphone)*: One moment, sir.

(Pause. Christmas Muzak wafts over the speakerphone for a moment.)

SYLVIA ZILINSKY *(Over speakerphone)*: Hello.

(Mizlansky looks to Brook in despair.)

MIZLANSKY *(Charming and thrilled)*: Sylvia? Is that *you*?

SYLVIA *(Over speakerphone)*: Hello, Davis.

MIZLANSKY: My God, how are you? I didn't know you were with Sam. What a surprise! Have you two had a little reconciliation?

(There is silence.)

SYLVIA *(Over speakerphone)*: Davis. Do me a favor. Sam just went to get some ice. He'll be back in a minute, so I'm going to speak to you openly and from the heart. Okay? Leave him alone.

MIZLANSKY: What—what are you doing there, Syl?

SYLVIA *(Over speakerphone)*: Hey, we may be divorced, but we still love each other. I came to him, because he needed me, he needed to talk. To be held. Because for all the stuff you guys do together, that you can't do. You should be thrilled, you won.

MIZLANSKY: I won?

SYLVIA *(Over speakerphone)*: You won, bubby. So walk away and let him go.

MIZLANSKY: Baby. You have the wrong idea. I care about his well-being. I—

SYLVIA *(Over speakerphone)*: Oh sweetie. Come on. I'm smart. I know the score. Now listen to me: your charm doesn't work on me. You know what you are? You are one of those pigs who gets dressed up on Halloween—*as a pig*—to fool everybody—but the truth is—Davis—we both know it—you're just a little Yiddish piglet from the *shtetl* who won.

MIZLANSKY *(Gentle)*: Okay. I won. But listen. It's a little late, Sylvia, for you to play protective wife, you know, forgive me, but you're hardly in a position to—as winner of the Martha Mitchell look-alike contest—a woman who walked out on Sam—

SYLVIA *(Over speakerphone, furious)*: Hey! Hey! Hey! I walked out because I couldn't get him away from you!

ZILINSKY *(Over speakerphone, away from the phone)*: Who is that? Is that *Davis*?

SYLVIA *(Over speakerphone, off but furious)*: Sam! If you speak to him I'm leaving. I'm not staying here while you let that—goddamn it, Sam!

(Sounds of a slight struggle and then the phone dropping.)

ZILINSKY *(Over speakerphone, off)*: Sylvia. Just wait. Just pour a drink and wait. By the pool. I'll be right out. Please. Please! Just wait!

(Mizlansky and Brook look at each other. Mizlansky shakes his head.)

ZILINSKY *(Into speakerphone)*: Davis?

MIZLANSKY: Well. Are you having a nice little reunion? *(Whispering)* Sam, don't give her any of the money, whatever you do, please, Sammy, listen to me. Don't give her the money!

ZILINSKY *(Over speakerphone)*: Take me off the speakerphone.

MIZLANSKY: Sammy? Sam? I got the telegram. Sammy. Sam. What is it?

ZILINSKY *(Over speakerphone)*: Take me off speakerphone.

MIZLANSKY: Do you mind, I'm eating, I haven't had a moment—

ZILINSKY *(Over speakerphone)*: Is someone with you?

MIZLANSKY: Jesus! No! Christ! Listen to yourself! Look. We need to settle this. I just want you to be happy. You can quit the business, you can keep the dough, but we need to be able to have a conversation so that I'm protected.

ZILINSKY *(Over speakerphone)*: I'm sure there's someone with you—

MIZLANSKY *(Soothing)*: Let's not do this on the phone. Let's sit down at Dupaars for some double-dip French toast and—

ZILINSKY *(Over speakerphone)*: I can't. I cannot be drawn into this! I didn't go into this business to be a crook. And I do not intend to protect you from that IRS guy. I'll tell them everything!

MIZLANSKY: Let's get together right now! I know that you function better face-to-face. Please! Come on, we'll go look at some galleries and some shoes.

ZILINSKY *(Over speakerphone, a strangled choke)*: Don't you get it, Davis? I'm scared of you! You scare me! Christ, you're—I can't get you out of my head, it's all Mizlansky crowding me out in here!

(There is the click of Sam hanging up. Then a dial tone. Mizlansky gets up and looks out over the canyon.)

MIZLANSKY: You have to have a particular nature, Miles, to be a whore. You know? And I always made this assumption that Sam had that in him—he could be turned out and made to perform—for his own good. Because some people are artists, some people are truly charismatic, have integrity, have passion, and he doesn't. He's just a smart, decent, weak man with good taste and bad judgment.

BROOK: Well, look, I would not be quite so respectful of his need for solitude right now: I'd get in Trecker's car and drive over there and settle this.

MIZLANSKY: Oh. Okay. I *see.* You want me to get in Trecker's orange VW Rabbit with the rust and the stickers and drive through Beverly Hills where there are people who just *watch* for—

TRECKER *(Entering with large tuna cans)*: Alan Tolkin is here, Davis. And I have the right tuna.

MIZLANSKY: That's not the right tuna. That's *Genoa* tuna, I need Florentine tuna. Because it has the right vitamins in the oil, Jesus, Paul, Paul, hey, man, can't you do the thing in a manner which is adult? The Florentine tuna has lipids in the oil which eat the plaque off your arteries, and by not getting me the right tuna you are committing attempted murder.

TRECKER: They-they-they-they-they—only had the tuna you said in the Italian—

MIZLANSKY *(Cutting him off, sweetly paternal)*: Look. Son. I'm not your daddy. I'm not your mommy. You work for me. Okay. Darling? Now, send in Mr. Tolkin.

BROOK: I don't mind taking Paul's car, and you can take mine if you don't mind—the roof won't—

MIZLANSKY: No! No! Paul needs his car to hunt down the correct items. He can't just sit here having a free day and chatting on the phone to his little Bohemian friends.

(Trecker exits, furious.)

BROOK: I'm going to talk to a friend at the IRS, see if I can find out anything. Maybe we can have him help us out . . . if I can offer him a little—

MIZLANSKY: Offer him anything! You have full offering power. Miles. You're a wonderful guy. And you have the one quality that will insure your success: loyalty. Loyalty to people.

(Trecker returns with Tolkin.)

Paul—you should learn from him. Miles—see if you—talk to the kid here—he stole my two Egyptian cats. I have a buyer who wants the pair! I have a buyer who's insane for bookends! And Trecker took them!

TRECKER: I did not! Stop with the cats already!

BROOK: Are you sure? You might have "forgotten."
TRECKER: No, no, *no*!

(Trecker exits with Brook.)

TOLKIN: Is this a bad time?
MIZLANSKY: Oh God, no. Finally a real grown-up. These people that I take care of with their broken wings, all the little broken-winged birdies who find their way to me.
TOLKIN: This house, it's so wonderful! It feels like Japan.
MIZLANSKY: It's my refuge, my place of meditation, it makes L.A. feel like—
TOLKIN *(Agreeing)*: Japan!
MIZLANSKY: Sedona! Open! Light! Hello, Alan. *(Beat)* I'm glad we ran into each other, and I'm heartbroken to hear that things are going not so well for you.
TOLKIN: I'm getting by. It's not, it's a slow—
MIZLANSKY: But what happened to all your projects?
TOLKIN: Well, they're still interested. I'm trying to do *Good Soldier Schwiek* with—it's very funny, it's comedy, if I can do it with Schwarzenegger, if I can get to him, also, you know, *The Golem*, he'd be great as the Golem, or even as a *Dybbuk*, the Yiddish canon—offers—with Schwarzenegger—
MIZLANSKY *(Bored to death, cuts him off)*: Oh yes, wonderful stuff, funny and warm and—but it's very hard. That's why I went into this tax-shelter business, it's an alternative to all the crazy craziness. *(Beat)* Look. It's great we ran into each other. I'd like you to come work on this thing with me. We need people with show-business names—it's for the prospectus—even though they're crappy little-kids' records—
TOLKIN: What would I do?
MIZLANSKY: Be an appraiser.
TOLKIN: An appraiser.
MIZLANSKY: Yes. How well do you know the Bible?
TOLKIN: Which book?
MIZLANSKY: Both testaments, first and second.

TOLKIN: Well, I don't—I took a Bible-as-literature class at Brandeis in the old days but—

MIZLANSKY: But that's all you need! Look at this.

(Mizlansky holds up a brightly colored album. "Revelation Revealed" in bold letters on the cover—with a cross between a comic-book superhero and an angel leaping over a flaming city in front of a mushroom cloud.)

MIZLANSKY: *Revelation Revealed!*

TOLKIN: What is that? An angel leaping over—

MIZLANSKY: It's an angel over L.A., which has been nuked—it's all about the cover art, they sell it at Kmart.

TOLKIN: It looks like the Riddler.

MIZLANSKY: It's *Gabriel! Revelation Revealed*—you know—a big title—anything with the word "Revelation" in the title—we sold about fifty different "Revelation" titles. It's a strangely popular book, these goyim love that crap—rules, baby. They all need rules.

TOLKIN: When you asked me to come over, I thought we could maybe—I thought you wanted to discuss movie projects . . .

MIZLANSKY: Oh, Jesus. Hey. You don't want me: I don't want to be a movie producer anymore! I hate that world! If I never have to walk into a studio again, I'd consider myself a home run! Look what it's done to you!

TOLKIN: I had a project I thought you'd appreciate: the hunt for Nazi war criminals in the U.S. I brought the treatment for it.

(He puts down a manila envelope. Mizlansky smiles.)

MIZLANSKY: Look. I love the way you've stuck it out, the way you have this weird social conscience, but sweetie, these people don't care about Nazis, they don't want a story, they don't want real! They don't want you!

TOLKIN: Perhaps my value system is out of whack.

MIZLANSKY: Don't talk about value systems in this area code.

Look at my dentist, Chick Dobleman, D.D.S. A brilliant man with a bicuspid, but he wanted to be a writer like his patients. He wanted to do an adaptation of—get this—get this one—Camus—*The Plague*—I swear to you!—and labored like some dental hygienist on that script, cleaning, scraping, polishing; finally, he gives up—he gives up in despair, and over Christmas, he's stuck in Bonwit's in line, gets this idea and writes *Slay Ride*, s-l-a-y ride, about a department-store Santa who goes berserk with a hatchet on Wilshire Boulevard. Huge, huge hit. So let's not talk about a town with a value system!

TOLKIN: He was *my* dentist, I know, but he had a breakdown. I'm not like him, I'm not ending up at Betty Ford eating yogurt, I'm a survivor—

MIZLANSKY: I'm saying "Move up!" This town, this world—is filled with the cautious, the bitter, the paralyzed, and I am offering you my hand in friendship—

TOLKIN: I have to check with my wife.

MIZLANSKY: Alan. I need an appraiser today. Someone with showbiz know-how whose opinion holds weight. We're in a real situation. Sam Zilinsky has blocked heart valves, he's got to rest.

TOLKIN: God. I'm sorry.

MIZLANSKY: This is my end-of-year crunch. I have six weeks of business left.

TOLKIN: You have two.

MIZLANSKY: Right! See how time flies? All you would do is sign the appraisal letters and meet a few buyers.

TOLKIN: I see.

MIZLANSKY: Look. You sign. And for every shelter we sell that has been appraised by you, you get two hundred dollars.

TOLKIN: So. You. What? You pay me if you sell the thing. Is that . . . ?

MIZLANSKY: I have two hundred letters for you to sign right now. There could be another two hundred along the way. So at very least, for this afternoon's work—you will walk away with forty thousand dollars. I *have* a buyer. Look. I don't want to sell you on this, Al. Okay. You want to be in the situation or you don't. If you do—you will—walk out of here with your self-respect and my gratitude and some nice friends.

TOLKIN: Tax shelters sound so—

MIZLANSKY: Scummy? Vulgar? *Sleazy?* Yes, they do! I agree! Who cares? Was anything we did in the service of making pictures any less scummy? Was it worth it to steal the studios' money—didn't you steal a Chrysler Le Baron when we had that deal at Fox? You *stole* their Chrysler; *that* wasn't such a problem?

TOLKIN: I didn't steal the Chrysler exactly, I just—when our deal was up I never gave it back because they never asked and—

MIZLANSKY: Please! I *approve* of what you did! I stole a Mustang. I stole everything that wasn't *nailed* down. For what? So that the guy at Musso Frank wouldn't make me wait for a table? Maybe I'm cursed with the blessing of self-awareness, but at least I am able to distinguish being a small-time grifter working the back lots from being my own boss and ripping off some hicks who hate paying taxes!

TOLKIN *(Numb)*: Yeah. No. Sure. Uh-huh. You're right. It's true. No. I agree. I should think about—

MIZLANSKY *(Softening)*: Look, maybe down the road we can find a way for the Nazi.

TRECKER *(Entering with more tuna cans, exhilarated)*: I got it! This is the right tuna!

MIZLANSKY *(Not bothering to look up)*: Is there a caper on the label?

TRECKER: No. There's a fig. I thought maybe *you*—maybe *you* got it wrong—

MIZLANSKY *(Patient as a kindergarten teacher)*: No. You see: I want the caper, not the fig, not the egg, not the chicken, Paul. The caper in extra-virgin Spanish olive oil from the Nuñez press in Seville—*Italian* tuna in *Spanish* oil, okay? Now go back and get the right one, okay, sweetie?

TRECKER *(After a beat)*: Okay. Uhm. Mr. De Vries is here.

MIZLANSKY: Okay. Seat him by the pool and offer him a smoothie and also, did you get that swivel-coupling thing for the vacuum?

TRECKER: I went to three places. They don't know what it is.

MIZLANSKY: You go to Mrs. Guptah on Ventura Boulevard at I Dream of Cleany. I don't want to explain this again. Call the Indian lady—she'll have it. The dust mites around here are getting in my eyes, and it's making me tear up, so, unless you want me *filled* with spores—

TRECKER: Okay. I'll—yeah—the Indian lady. But she said—

MIZLANSKY: No she didn't. She didn't say *anything*. Don't lie before you speak, lie *after* you speak, okay?

TRECKER: Okay. I won't. That's very good advice.

MIZLANSKY: Don't suck up to me. Do the job. You're not getting anything special for sucking up. God! Any news on the car?

TRECKER: Achmed called. He's almost there.

MIZLANSKY: What happened? Did his camel die?

(Handing Trecker the outline.)

I want a report from you on Mr. Tolkin's Nazi treatment by tonight.

TRECKER *(Looking at it, then at him)*: You want a synopsis of a treatment? Could it *be* any shorter?

MIZLANSKY: Hey. I want coverage. *Full* coverage. Has my daughter called?

TRECKER: She wants her check. She's very angry.

MIZLANSKY: What do you mean "she's very angry"? Being angry is an *action*, and that would require *effort*, it would actually take *work* to be angry, which would take time away from eating and screwing and *getting her masters in break dancing*! How come you were friends with her? Was it because it was a way to get to me?

TRECKER *(After a beat)*: Yes.

MIZLANSKY *(Laughing)*: I love it when you're ironic, kid. If you stay ironic you'll run this town. Man. Will you run it, if you learn not to make my mistakes, my animosity which got in my way, you'll run this town . . . Now—go! The vacuum and the tuna!—the *ultimate* porn title! And please, the joke with the cats has gone too far, it was funny, now it's not. Give them back. Please. This buyer isn't going to wait forever!

(Silence. Trecker leaves. Mizlansky sighs.)

MIZLANSKY: Look. Alan. I have a man sitting by the pool. He is an investment counselor from Enid, Oklahoma, representing a consortium of dentists. This is the guy. He is looking for two hundred titles. And I don't have them. *Until* I have a letter of appraisal. I need your name.

(Mizlansky holds out a sheaf of documents. Tolkin takes it.)

TOLKIN *(Reading)*: "As an expert in the field of family-entertainment marketing, I have seen several remarkable products, but in my opinion very seldom has any product had the potential to perform as well as the Old Brompton Corporation recording of *Somethin's Happenin' in Jerusalem* . . ." *(Beat) Is* it good? Should I listen to it?

MIZLANSKY: It's fine. You have to understand, in this business the standards are different—mediocre is excellent. But there are two hundred titles, you can't listen to them all! He's waiting.

TOLKIN: But why me?

MIZLANSKY: Alan. We go back. You were my line producer twice. Come on. Let me give you this.

(He takes an envelope out of the desk drawer. Puts it on the table.)

Here. A signing bonus. Count it. Cash. Five grand. Just for saying yes. Just for being here in this room when Mr. Horton De Vries from Enid, Oklahoma, walks in. Just for being polite! Five thousand dollars for driving up the canyon. *(Beat)* See? It's going to be a marvelous Christmas!

TOLKIN: I guess I've said yes, haven't I?

(Tolkin starts to sign the letters.)

MIZLANSKY: "Yes" is a word that brings riches. "No" is a word that brings tears. *(Into speakerphone)* Send in Mr. De Vries, Paul. *(Pause)* Now. Alan. Be yourself. If he makes you nervous, excuse yourself. In the bathroom there is a vial of Xanax in a bottle marked Lomotil. They dissolve sublingually in about thirty-six seconds.

DE VRIES *(Entering)*: Davis! Davis!

MIZLANSKY *(Solemn)*: Horton. The Oklahoma Money Maniac! You're here!

DE VRIES: What a magnificent place! I was sitting out in the garden, you've got the most beautiful koi fish!

MIZLANSKY: Do you like koi?

DE VRIES: We have a pond! We keep losing the poor things—

MIZLANSKY *(Into speakerphone)*: Paul. I want you to put the biggest fish we have—catch him, put him in a baggy and pack him up for Mr. De Vries.

TRECKER *(Over intercom)*: Uhm, do I—

MIZLANSKY: Get in the *pond* and use the *net*!

DE VRIES: That's very kind, but I'm going from L.A. to Miami and Traverse City—and I couldn't take your biggest—

MIZLANSKY: I love Traverse City! My friend: these are Mizlansky koi; they are sturdy—you could travel with these goldfish to Beirut, swim 'em around in the Red Sea, they'd be fine. Take the fish. I need you to take the fish! As a symbol of our unity and besides—the fish—

TOLKIN: —is the symbol of Christianity, is he not?

(There is a moment. Mizlansky beams.)

DE VRIES *(Moved)*: Thank you. Thank you very much.

MIZLANSKY: Now. This is my glorious friend Alan Tolkin, our star appraiser, who worked with me on several of the pictures in the old days. He has since gone on, let me tell you, to great things in television movies. He produced *Without My Father*, that movie about children who—

DE VRIES *(Over this)*: Did you work on *Sidewinder Summer?*

MIZLANSKY: Not only did he work on it, he wrote it *and* was the unit publicist!

DE VRIES: Well, it's a thrill to meet all these creative artists!

MIZLANSKY: Your meeting with my partner, Sam, in New York went well?

DE VRIES: Golly; I love the guy! What a wonderful man! He's so learned! Such sophistication! I just never get to meet folks like him! My clients are so excited—I've been making calls—explaining what you boys have come up with—and frankly, they're thrilled. They are so sick of oil wells! Because it's dangerous! You could actually hit crude! The well could be a gusher and then what?

MIZLANSKY: I can assure you, the children's Bible stories are not gushers. They are not even tricklers. But the secret lies in positioning their potential in the marketplace in such a way so as to convey the faint and distinct hint of profitability somewhere down the line. In a dreamy alternate universe.

(Pause. De Vries picks up one of the letters of appraisal. He reads.)

DE VRIES: It's a very good product. No doubt. The only thing I worry about is how you—you have here on the letter of appraisal—you think a recording of the story of the Last Supper, with the voice of Flip Wilson, you think that master recording is worth a quarter of a million dollars over twenty-five years . . . ?

MIZLANSKY: TWENTY-FIVE *YEARS!* A quarter century! It's the Bible. It's—

TOLKIN: An evergreen.

MIZLANSKY: It has staying power. A presence. It's not a game of Pong. Theoretically—that is the key word—"theoretical"—the product could perform very well over twenty-five years, sure—will it? If I answered that yes—you would leave—

TOLKIN *(Gathering confidence)*: It's a story. It will have value that outlasts computer games and oil wells. It speaks to children. It speaks to family. It speaks to home. To *home.*

MIZLANSKY: Is it so unreasonable to assume that a treasure such as this would not be worth a quarter of a million dollars over a quarter of a century, sir?

TOLKIN: The Bible never goes out of style.

(Mizlansky glances at Tolkin, an appreciative smile.)

MIZLANSKY: Amen.

DE VRIES: I can't have the IRS hunting my clients down. In a year or in three years. These men go hunting.

MIZLANSKY: Understand. My counsel, Miles Brook, has been consulting with tax attorneys in Delaware. Last year, we won the PTA Award in Louisville and Lafayette for responsible children's recordings—the Duck Award.

DE VRIES: I just have to tell the boys back home what we've got to look forward to. I want to make this deal. Now, in your prospectus, it says something about getting involved in some of your motion-picture projects—see—that's something my folks would find sexy.

MIZLANSKY: Well. We're currently involved in a very exciting project. *Wolf at the Door: The Hunt for Nazi War Criminals in the U.S.*

DE VRIES: I see. The hunt. I'm sure they'd be interested, except for Doctor Vlaukhausen . . .

MIZLANSKY: Frankly, this is not something I'm comfortable discussing at this stage, 'cause things get swiped in this town, but I will say this: it's a serious subject. A nightmare. War criminals. Posing! Posing as regular people! We found a kid from Harvard who worked at the State Department, he has an extraordinary sense of the historical context—he knows the Holocaust backwards and forwards and was electrified into action.

DE VRIES *(Sighing deeply)*: Nazis. Nazis. Nazis. My, my, my.

MIZLANSKY: Apparently they're swarming all over: Wisconsin? Madison is full of them.

DE VRIES: It's the kind of story that doesn't go away.

TOLKIN: It has an *urgency*.

MIZLANSKY: See, Horton: protection from the tax man is easy. But what isn't so simple is to find a world that is vibrating with possibility, that is meaningful, that gives you pride. That's what we're about at Mizlansky/Zilinsky: pride. The pride of being a part of something glorious.

DE VRIES: You know, I do wish one more thing: you had more names of show-business folk on your letterhead; the more legitimacy you can show my clients, the better.

MIZLANSKY: Legitimacy.

DE VRIES: Credibility. Hollywood glitter.

MIZLANSKY: Well, you mean like a star or something?

DE VRIES: That would be just about right. A real Hollywood star.

(Pause.)

MIZLANSKY: My friend. We have had to turn stars away from this, because, frankly, sometimes they're a little hard to handle, they need special water, a room with special lighting, they make you buy clothes, they try and seduce your kids, they are rude to your wife, but hey, if it's a star you need on the Mizlansky/Zilinsky letterhead, if it's a star that will close this deal, a star you will get.

DE VRIES: Could you get Strother Martin? I loved that movie, *Ssss!*

MIZLANSKY: Strother is a very good friend, he lives one canyon over.

DE VRIES: Or Darren McGavin.

MIZLANSKY: He goes to my gym.

DE VRIES: That Van Patten fellow from the boat?

MIZLANSKY: I saw him at Nate 'N' Al on line on Wednesday. He was number fifty-one, he's probably still waiting. I've got his number here. You know who I've got to call—I've got to call Shecky.

DE VRIES: Perhaps you could get someone who is not quite so ethnic.

MIZLANSKY *(Dangerous)*: Ethnic?

DE VRIES: It's not me.

MIZLANSKY: Oh.

DE VRIES: Just—some of the clients—not me—I just want to balance the—it's not *me*—

MIZLANSKY *(Calm)*: I understand. Horton. We know you're not saying anything.

TOLKIN *(Almost hysterical)*: Huh.

DE VRIES *(Standing to go)*: I think if you were to deliver. To *get* an endorsement from a personality, that would go a long way—give me a star, an *American* star I can *display* for my clients, a John Wayne, a John Gavin, and I can virtually assure you, I will give you the Enid and Tulsa Medical Financial Planning and Investing Group to do with as you wish.

MIZLANSKY: Well. Good. Because I love an easy deal.

DE VRIES: Then I'll call tomorrow and we can get rolling on the paperwork . . .

MIZLANSKY: Yeah.

DE VRIES: And of course, Sam Zilinsky, he'll be here?

MIZLANSKY: Well. We're hoping! He's had a very busy time of it. The New York clients! So pushy! They need this, they need that. He's intending to get here, but we might be on our own.

DE VRIES: I just think that it's always better that all parties be in the same room, with this kind of deal. I have found that it just works better that way, so there's no misunderstandings . . .

MIZLANSKY: Right. My God, do I agree! Please.

DE VRIES: With money changing hands . . . we have cashier's checks. Cash . . . we have all those signatures, we have—we want to be on the same page . . . We really want Sam to be here.

MIZLANSKY *(Cheerful, ushering De Vries out)*: Say no more. You want to be comfortable, I get it.

(Trecker enters, wordlessly, carrying a plastic baggy filled with water. It houses a koi fish. Trecker is quite wet. He hands it to De Vries and exits.)

DE VRIES: Good to meet you, Al, I'm sure we'll be seeing more of each other in the weeks to come. I have to get back to my hotel, I'm taking my wife to the Olvera Tar Pits. Y'all have a nice day now, ya hear.

(He exits. A silence.)

TOLKIN: God, what was that aftershave he had on?

MIZLANSKY: I didn't notice, I have septum trouble, but did it smell like lychee nuts? *All* these guys smell like lychee nuts. They can't make a deal without smelling sweet. *(Beat)* You were great just now.

TOLKIN *(Outraged, interrupts)*: You heard that thing he—that— what he said about—"ethnic"? Please—it's years since I heard that shit.

MIZLANSKY: Yeah. Look. *(Beat)* Hey. Your best friend, the guy who was on the series for a while, the guy who had a drinking problem? Tintoretto?

TOLKIN: Lionel? Lionel Hart? He's been sober for years.

MIZLANSKY: Yeah. Let's get him. He's a name. He'll do.

TOLKIN *(Laughing)*: Lionel Hart? Lionel Hartstein? Whose father was the cantor at Temple Beit Emanuel in *Williamsburg?* That Lionel Hart?

MIZLANSKY: Just get him, he played a detective on TV, it cancels out that he's Jewish, he's fine, get him, and I'll give you another signing bonus plus twenty for him. I need his name on the menu.

TOLKIN: Davis. Please. Really. Be blunt. Tell me: is this business, are these shelters going to be trouble in any way? Down the road?

MIZLANSKY: What do you think? It's the gray area. That's where this lives. It lives in the gray. Trouble is sometimes hard to define—

TOLKIN: But am I—dragging in Lionel—who is—an actor—a public guy—*weak*—but a person with a *name*—is he . . . ? At risk of . . . ? A kind of exposure to . . . ?

MIZLANSKY: An *unemployed* actor, if I remember correctly, an unemployed actor who does plays in L.A. *for a living*! On *Melrose*! If I remember! Molière at Equity Waiver? Is that the man we're talking about?

TOLKIN: He's my friend! He's my partner on several projects!

MIZLANSKY: Well, maybe you should look at that. Hey. I know what it means to carry someone: I'm carrying Zilinsky right now! I'm sympathetic to loyalty, I'm offering you a chance to do a favor for a floundering friend.

TOLKIN: Don't underestimate his talent. Last summer Lionel Hart played Prospero in Oregon at the Bardathon, he was wonderful, you should have seen—he got a new agent out of it, he's about to—he's up for a bunch of things—big things—he's—he's . . .

MIZLANSKY *(Kindly)*: He's dead as cold mutton, Alan. Isn't he? So am I. And so are you. The only one who isn't is Mr. Horton De Vries of the Oklahoma Klan. I'm sorry. But here we are. "Is it illegal?" Who gives a fuck if it's illegal or not, the question is how much more of this life can you take? How much more? *(Beat)* Aren't you tired? I'm so tired. I just want to get my money and get out.

(Pause. Tolkin nods. Mizlansky shrugs casually.)

MIZLANSKY: He would be playing host. He'd meet the Oklahomans and eat with them and his name would be on the prospectus and he'd narrate a few chapters and verses.

TOLKIN *(Beaten)*: I'll go see him, Davis.

MIZLANSKY: Talk to him about hope. Tell him I offer it at ten percent below cost, which is considerably better than any of his "new agents" will do.

(Tolkin walks out, nodding. Mizlansky stands in the quiet sunlit room, worn down. He hits the speakerphone.)

MIZLANSKY: Paul. What's the word on my car?

TRECKER *(On speakerphone)*: I just called the shop. They don't know where Achmed is.

MIZLANSKY: They don't know where Achmed is? Hey! I need my car! I have Sam going nuts on me! I need my car, this is crazy, maybe he stole it, the guy is from Baghdad, my Mercedes is probably on some magic carpet back to Persia by now!

TRECKER: Davis. Just take mine.

MIZLANSKY: The little orange thing? Well, thank you very much, Cinderella, but I won't be needing the pumpkin. Go down the hill and wait with my car!

(Longish pause.)

TRECKER *(Over speakerphone)*: You're mean.

(Mizlansky clicks off. A moment. He turns on the radio to a California, light rock radio station, and crosses to the stationery bicycle. He mounts the bike and pedals to the music with sudden ferocity. He cries. Trecker appears and spies on him for a moment, watching with a mixture of pity and contempt. Mizlansky notices him and stops pedaling, suddenly self-conscious.)

TRECKER: You okay?

MIZLANSKY: God, I'd love some Hunan food. Let's eat.

(Blackout.)

SCENE 3

6:15 P.M. Mizlansky's living room. The late-afternoon light has shifted the shadows, and the sky has gone L.A. red. Mizlansky, Brook and Trecker eating expensive Chinese takeout from cartons, using chopsticks and drinking expensive ginger beer in fancy bottles. All of them eat throughout the scene.

MIZLANSKY *(His mouth full, shrugging, mid-explanation)*: Well. They don't know what they've—they always make noise— but then they don't have anything concrete and can't afford to—

BROOK *(Very agitated)*: Look, Davis—my friend knows what's going on. If he says the IRS has decided to put a task force on "small shelter promoters" and that means *you*—then they're gearing up: they don't wait until *after* the holi- days—they go full steam ahead *with* the cooperation of the Securities and Exchange people. Okay? Right?

(Beat.)

MIZLANSKY: The timing. Can you believe it? Does your friend think Firnbach can be bought?

BROOK: No. He doesn't! He's very—Firnbach went to Yeshiva— according to my friend he's fanatical—a zealot about taxes—

MIZLANSKY *(Moaning)*: Can't—we—have your friend show him how much I give to—

BROOK: It doesn't *matter*. Firnbach doesn't care about charity. He's coming after you hard!

MIZLANSKY: I've got to keep Sam on track.

BROOK: But I don't think he's stable, he's not going to be able to hold his own—I think that what will happen—is there a napkin? The IRS guy, Firnbach will focus on him 'cause he's so weak—so what I'm proposing is we make a deal with him—a deal where he moves to France.

MIZLANSKY: He moves to France?

TRECKER: *I'd* like to move to France.

MIZLANSKY: Shut up.

BROOK: We give Sam a percent of the business. You escort him—a one-way ticket to Paris—on the Concorde, you'll be back in a day.

MIZLANSKY: He'll never do it—

BROOK: He'll talk to Firnbach any day, he'll cut a deal with them and turn you in—it's just a matter of time—

MIZLANSKY: He may be a—you know what, Trecker? Would you mind walking down the hill again? How long can it take to repair a car? I mean, what are they—maybe they're having a little Arab tea party. Also I left a sweater which I'm sure they'll take—

TRECKER *(Seething)*: No. Please. They're in the middle—they said they'd drive it up here when they were done! Achmed promised. Another few minutes.

MIZLANSKY *(Eating)*: I've got to get down there. God, I love these smoked dried red peppers—on the squid.

TRECKER *(Mouth full)*: It's a special dried chili from Hunan. The chef there toasts them in a Mandarin smoker. He uses mesquite, so it gives it a special, delicate, woody infusion.

MIZLANSKY: Hey, Paul, can I ask you a question? Are you just a little bit gay?

TRECKER: Yes. I am. I'm not pretending—I never said I wasn't!

MIZLANSKY *(While chewing, a sudden agitation evident)*: No you're not gay! Don't say that, please don't be gay, we don't need more gay Jewish guys running around Beverly Hills, buying little Italian sweaters and espadrilles, just, can't you get your pee-pee untwisted and go straight? Please, I swear, if I hear you're going to David Geffen's and Barry Diller's house for "pool parties" I'll fire you.

TRECKER: If I were going to their pool parties, I would most certainly not be working for you, pal.

MIZLANSKY *(A mouthful of food)*: Hey, you know what? With Sam and me at least you can laugh; with those guys you could never joke around.

OOK: Yeah.

MIZLANSKY: You don't appreciate—either of you—Miles—this man has been a real friend, I'm not just going to cut him loose here—I've had my bad moments and he's seen me through—let me tell you something: this is a man who could make a deal without making a deal. You wouldn't know he was selling! He honestly had a way of taking the grime off a negotiation and making it elegant. You guys think it's all me? It's not. I have energy. Big deal. It's—he has—he's the one with the touch. It's a big secret.

TRECKER: He bought me a dictionary last year which had pictures of things and all their correct proper names. Real names. Like little weird things which you would never even know had a name, parts of a shoe or a rake or a plant. A pictorial dictionary. I spend hours looking at it. Sometimes at night I stare at it.

MIZLANSKY: Look up "chiropodist." *(Beat)* I'll tell you. Sam is worth the trouble. Is the thing. Some people are hard work, not easy, like me. This is a man who had an eye—he could—his taste—if all it took to run a studio was great taste, this man would have been Jack Warner, David Selznick and Lew Wasserman all rolled into one. He knew hippies were the next thing before they got big, he knew bike pictures were going to hit, he knew when beach pictures were over before anybody. I always thought "Why is he sticking with me? He could do anything." *(Beat)* Hey— you know what? I can't wait for the car anymore. I'll walk down the hill! Okay! Jesus!

(The phone rings. Mizlansky looks at Trecker, who has a mouth full of food too.)

I'm not here! Unless it's Achmed or Sam!

BROOK: If it's the IRS, tell them to call back later!

TRECKER *(Into phone)*: Hello, Mizlansky residence.

ESTHER *(Over speakerphone)*: Paul? Put Davis on, I know he's there.

I drove by on my way to Pilates class. I saw him scrunching around in the living room like the rat he is.

MIZLANSKY *(Defeated)*: Hi, Esther. What can I do for you, my darling? It's been a long time!

ESTHER *(Over speakerphone, sweetly)*: I have one question for you: are you in big trouble, Davis?

MIZLANSKY: Excuse me?

ESTHER *(Over speakerphone)*: Davis. Trecker walked right into my apartment and stole my Christo sculpture.

(Mizlansky looks at Trecker and sighs. Trecker looks helpless.)

MIZLANSKY *(Deadpan)*: Your Christo sculpture, did you say?

ESTHER *(Over speakerphone)*: Yeah, the *Wrapped Brick*. Now. Honey. Not only have you not paid alimony for eight months, but now you are sending the kid sneaking into my home and ransacking. Understand. My neighbor Mrs. Moji-gan Tagzenaygee actually witnessed this. So denial is futile. Now you do not know this, but I have had to go to work at Neiman Marcus—spraying ladies with—spraying innocent girls with some sort of eau de cologne which smells like a banana-lime dessert from the cheesecake factory! And this I do for three dollars and twenty-six cents an hour. And I do not mind it! Because it's better than having to fight you for my money.

(Pause. Silence.)

Davis? I take it that your silence is affirmation. Good. Okay. So keep the money for the Christo, I'm sure you sold it already, and forget the back alimony, but remember; when you lie in bed, your throat swollen with allergies, and your head bursting and your hiatal hernia pounding and some gal is pouting beside you, remember me, and you're rich again but it feels like there's something gritty in your eye, remember me and send over a check, okay, pal?

(Pause. There are the sounds of ice clinking in a glass and a cigarette being lit.)

Because I can keep working at Neiman's for as long as it takes, if I know that I'm your one little shot at decency. And when you do send over a check, double it, okay? Double what your instinct tells you. On the big day, when the big pay-off finally comes in, I want you to say, "Half goes to Esther, for the sake of my soul." Be the Davis Mizlansky who did one *slightly* impressive thing because if you don't . . . what will you have?

MIZLANSKY *(Softly, weepy, hypnotized)*: Okay, Esther. Okay. "Half goes to Esther."

ESTHER *(Over speakerphone, softly)*: That's a good boy, Davis. Now. Davis, believe me, if you screw me, I'm gonna send some boys from Kiev over to see you, some kids from the south side of Beverly Hills, and you know, the only thing they like more than a plate of pierogi is breaking a leg.

(There is the click of a hang-up from the other end. Then a dial tone. Mizlansky reaches over and flicks off the speakerphone. He turns away from Trecker and Brook. There is silence. Then the ringing of the doorbell.)

TRECKER *(Softly, rising)*: I'll get it.

(He exits. Mizlansky wipes away a tear. Mizlansky sniffles. Brook is embarrassed. Trecker returns.)

MIZLANSKY *(Heartbroken)*: She always believed in me. Unlike all the other people in my life, she believed in me the way Pat believed in Dick . . . and I've killed her, selling perfume . . .

TRECKER *(Low and serious)*: It's a Mr. Firnbach. From the IRS. He's in the foyer. He won't leave until he sees you guys.

MIZLANSKY *(Suddenly calm and cool and mercenary)*: Miles. Take care of him, string him out. Paul, offer him a plate of that Hunan chicken, make sure you give him a lot of those chilies, nothing to drink, if he asks, tell him the water's been turned off, don't give him a drink. I'm going to slip out the back, go down the hill and see Zilinsky before he sells us down the River Styx. *(Beat)* Trecker: give me the keys to your Rabbit.

(Blackout.)

Act Two

ZILINSKY

7:30 P.M. That evening. The veranda of a poolside room at the Hotel Casa de la Ventana del Sol on Wilshire. The suggestion of a swimming pool nearby. Sam Zilinsky is dressed in casual Italian country-gentleman's clothing; very expensive stuff; close-cropped gray hair, horn-rimmed glasses.)

MIZLANSKY: Good God, it's a flophouse! It's a suicide hotel! Sam! The colors! You have the Irwin Allen suite!

ZILINSKY *(Smiling, shrugs)*: Expensive cheap hotels on the fringe of luxury. Where I am most comfortable, Davis.

MIZLANSKY: It's very depressing. Can't you do better than this?

ZILINSKY *(Laughing)*: You think real life is depressing. You think unless there is no trace at all of real human effort, it's shabby.

(There is a moment. Zilinsky offers Mizlansky a cigar. They smoke.)

MIZLANSKY: So. Kiddo. What? You what? You flew to Grand Cayman. Bought some Havanas. Went to our little bank on the beach, you *withdraw the dough*, but what do you think while you're doing it? I just want to know? Standing there on Cayman Beach with an Asprey bag filled with my money.

ZILINSKY: Yours? But of course, it's all yours, isn't it, Davis? *(With great relish)* I thought, "it's not *much*, but I can live on it. If I have to run. I can live. *Just*. I can move to Mexico, say, to San Miguel de Allende, and live quite nicely on the interest off a quarter of a million. I'm free. *Finally*."

MIZLANSKY: What with the peso and all, sure, a sort of Bohemian grandeur, a *certain squalid expatriate romance*, right? Of course, if you make a deal with the government, you don't have to run, do you? Listen, pal, you're in the middle of a nice big sloppy nervous breakdown, and I'm not going to get in the way, except I can't let you hurt yourself.

ZILINSKY: I promise you, I'm not having a breakdown, Davis. I actually feel, actually—really—pretty good. I feel like I'm breaking free.

MIZLANSKY: Free? Of?

ZILINSKY: Why—you. Of course.

MIZLANSKY: I did not realize I exerted such a pull.

ZILINSKY *(Laughing)*: I can't even have this discussion with you.

MIZLANSKY: Why not?

ZILINSKY: My dear Davis: you really don't want to hear me analyze our relationship.

MIZLANSKY: I thought it was a *friendship*. I didn't realize it was a "relationship." I thought we were "best friends."

ZILINSKY: Yes. But. What does that mean to you? Does it mean you can bully, dictate, lie to, manipulate . . . ?

MIZLANSKY: This is, Sam, this is such an embarrassment to our—

ZILINSKY: To our what?

MIZLANSKY: To our manhood, for one. It's so female, this thing you're drawing me into; men do not have this talk.

ZILINSKY: Men don't talk about their "relationships"?

MIZLANSKY: It's vulgar. It's unseemly.

ZILINSKY: To talk about feelings makes you nervous?

MIZLANSKY: It makes me sick, frankly. It feels dirty.

ZILINSKY: It feels dirty to talk of feelings? It feels sticky? It feels . . . ?

MIZLANSKY: With you, *filthy*.

ZILINSKY: Interesting. Because—well, Doctor Belami thinks that you're a homosexual, so I can see why you might find this discussion threatening.

MIZLANSKY: I'm a homosexual?

ZILINSKY: You are a particular type of nonactive *emotional* homosexual who preys on the affections of men who have fraternal instincts, yes.

MIZLANSKY *(Bewildered)*: Fraternal? Fraternal instincts! Who do you think you are?

ZILINSKY: The actual notion of a homosexual encounter is repulsive but the primary drive you have is toward your own gender. Doctor Belami has been very helpful on this point.

MIZLANSKY: The primary drive? I want to fuck a guy?

ZILINSKY: Bingo!

MIZLANSKY: And who, pray, is Doctor Belami? Some Park Avenue seer, no doubt, filled with a magical Viennese wisdom?

ZILINSKY: Doctor Belami is no joke. Doctor Belami escaped Buchenwald and has saved half of Broadway single-handedly—he virtually eliminated the problem of stage fright.

MIZLANSKY: How unfortunate. But. More important than the problem of stage fright: does Doctor Belami think you are a homosexual too?

ZILINSKY *(Beat. Smiling)*: Doctor Belami thinks everyone is a homosexual. But the issue—the issue of escaping the oppression of a relationship with someone who is *stronger*—

MIZLANSKY: And which one of us is that?

ZILINSKY: *You*, of course.

MIZLANSKY: *Me*, of course?

ZILINSKY: *Obviously*!

MIZLANSKY: Really?

ZILINSKY *(Exasperated)*: Yes! My *God*! You, Davis Mizlansky; the Toad of Toad Hall of Beverly Hills! You are a psychosexual hysteric, a looting, pillaging anarchist, Davis, who has operated on the edges, like Peter Lorre in *M*, but charming others into your—

MIZLANSKY *(Fierce)*: *That's* what you think? That I am the bully? That I'm the maniac? That I am the pusher, that I am the force of nature? Well. Have we ever—leaving aside the—let's put aside the thing about being a homosexualist for a moment—let's put aside how *offensive* and *dumb* and *creepy* that is, let's shunt that off to one side and examine the many ways in which *you* dominate *me*!

ZILINSKY *(After a moment)*: Me? Me dominate you? Are you crazy? Do you know what you've done to me? I'm a *Watergate* character because of you! Because of you I'm verging on "unindicted coconspirator" status, *if I'm lucky!*

MIZLANSKY: No! Let us talk about one-upmanship. Let's talk about the problem of green suede oxfords. Where did you get them?

ZILINSKY *(Suspicious)*: Tokyo.

MIZLANSKY: Exactly. You got your shoes in Tokyo! Now. The way this normally works is, you wear the shoes, I see them and go crazy, call Tokyo, and they don't have them—ever again! And yet—you continue to wear them—to torture me—so that I then try and have them copied without you knowing—at great cost and with only satisfactory results.

ZILINSKY *(A shrug)*: It's crazy, I have style, having style is not a sin, it's hard work, and if you need to copy that, *fine*, I hardly see where in the story I impose my—

MIZLANSKY *(Cuts him off)*: No, of course not. Because *that* is what you do. With all your leisure time, you shop for things to make me jealous, you read obscure literature, you make friends with academics—all things done to make me jealous—

ZILINSKY *(A slow burn)*: I see. I see. I see. Such as?

MIZLANSKY: A long list. English facial products. Swiss ties. Who ever heard of *Swiss* ties? Leather goods from Montenegro? These fabrics you have, which bespeak so much ease! Caviar from little seaside villages in Iran. A restaurant in Redondo Beach that nobody knows about! A new novel about a witty Italian talking *cat* who lives, *I don't know*, in someone's *rectum*; a this, a that! Every day there was something else. I sweat trying to keep up!

ZILINSKY: This is poisonous childishness of the first order!

MIZLANSKY: *Plus*: I have deduced the following! Your move to New York was all about access to Barney's. New York means nothing to you other than culinary gorging! It was about access to *matzoh-breih*, dinner parties and beautiful fall days, which you would report gleefully! Anything I could not have access to, stuck out here in this smog swamp, you wanted!

ZILINSKY: My move to New York was an attempt to get away from—

MIZLANSKY: Fine: let's talk about literature. Books! Pretending to read these things, pretending to read *biographies* merely to have something ghastly to hold over my head! To make me feel like some horrible little illiterate troll under a bridge—

ZILINSKY: This is your sickness! This is the hostility of a man who hates anyone whom he thinks might have had some sort of advantage—

MIZLANSKY: *Advantage*? *Privilege*? Because, yes, I pulled myself up out of the south side of Chicago and did not graduate high school, yes, I grew up across the street from Saul Bellow who never even smiled at me! Yes, and became my own boss in a world of pigs! Because we know that the world out here is one of pigs in heat!

ZILINSKY: Look. I know a really nice Egyptian shrink in Echo Park. She's smart, she's attractive, she'll get to the bottom of your pathological competitive *mania* and—

MIZLANSKY *(Quiet)*: Please. *Enough*. Look. Look at what you're reading, here by the pool of a Wilshire Boulevard motel!

(He picks up a book. Laughs.)

The Collected Letters of Horace Walpole, Fourth Earl of Orford . . . Now come on. Really. Look . . . You've proven my point.

ZILINSKY: Walpole is not a joke! His survey of English art is standard. It is the standard text on the development of—

(Zilinsky watches Mizlansky revel in his laughter.)

MIZLANSKY: You're like some kind of Park Avenue Jewish WASP: where's your yacht? . . . I mean, come on. *Please*. Concede the point that this is absurd! Man! This holds no conceivable interest to who you really are!

ZILINSKY *(After a moment of calm)*: I concede the point. Yes. To read Walpole at the pool of the Casa de la Ventana del Sol on Wilshire is absurd. But Davis. It's over. Because you are just a . . . cancer to my soul, even though I love you.

MIZLANSKY *(Nods. Thinks for a moment)*: I've been a damn good friend to you. I believe. Like spending a fortune optioning Spiro Agnew's life story. I've been a good friend! If I am not rewriting too much history.

ZILINSKY: You think you have.

MIZLANSKY: I know it.

ZILINSKY: Perhaps you know me too well. Perhaps I know *you* too well. Maybe to be known so well, it's too much. To be seen so . . . I can't . . . bear that. The scrutiny . . .

MIZLANSKY: Look. Let's put all this emotion in the closet. We have practical issues here: the deal with De Vries . . .

ZILINSKY: Yes. But I'm sorry. There is no going back.

MIZLANSKY: Have you talked yet?

ZILINSKY: What do you mean?

MIZLANSKY: To the IRS? Have you whined and seduced and blabbed to Mr. Firnbach?

ZILINSKY: I don't know how much longer I can hold back. They're promising me immunity if I cooperate! They have us dead to rights on backdating, on fraud.

MIZLANSKY: Listen; They have *nothing*! They have *conjecture*! There is no way they can prove any of it—*listen* to me— Sam. Sam. Help me close the De Vries deal, and you walk away with at least a few million. My God! It's half written, the check is half written, sitting there, waiting!

ZILINSKY: Oh, God. Davis, no.

MIZLANSKY: Go out with a little class, buddy. You have a choice!

ZILINSKY: Too late for that.

MIZLANSKY: Sam. You owe me something. This is the last chance I will ever have to make any money—look around—look around—how much longer will this kind of L.A. exist? All these little hotels here on Wilshire—they're being turned into Lexington Avenue. Our L.A. is evaporating.

ZILINSKY: Listen to yourself! You're not an old man, you're going to do something else, you'll be fine.

MIZLANSKY: No. Don't you understand the concept of "burning out"? Everything is changing! We are not up-to-date people, Sam! There's no place for what we do! We have to do this deal!

ZILINSKY *(Calm)*: This is what you do: you do this Dostoyevskian panic dance of death where it's the end of the world, and you drag everyone down with you, Davis. It's not healthy. It's not a healthy way to live! I can't. *(Beat)* Do you want to know what else? Doctor Belami told me that I have something called Feline Flight-or-Fight Syndrome.

MIZLANSKY *(Bewildered)*: What? What are you talking about? Feline *what?*

ZILINSKY: Feline Flight-or-Fight Syndrome! Cats get it when they're upset and don't know what to do! *Cats* get it! When they can't figure out whether to run or fight—their blood pressure soars and their adrenaline starts pumping! I have this! Because of you!

(Beat.)

MIZLANSKY: You have something cats get?

ZILINSKY: I have a feline disorder!

(Pause.)

MIZLANSKY: Sam. Let me explain this to you: you walk away from this thing, and there's nothing left. We were kids when we got out here, we were at our peak when we were twenty-two years old. The new generation, the new mailroom kids, they look like they never sleep, they never have any fun, and I've run out of ideas!

ZILINSKY: Well, I don't need as much as you, buddy. I don't need a "last deal."

MIZLANSKY: The money you stole. It was all I had! Everything else has gone into the business.

ZILINSKY: We both know that is a lie. We both know you have something hidden somewhere. *(Beat, unsure)* Don't you?

MIZLANSKY: I *honestly* don't. I pillaged myself. Nothing. Please, Sammy! Help me close this, and you are on the next flight out. It's my last deal!

ZILINSKY: Davis, you're an addict. This is morphine to you.

MIZLANSKY: I'm on my knees.

ZILINSKY: No you're not.

MIZLANSKY: In my heart, I am.

(Pause. Zilinsky looks at the pool. The sun beats down.)

MIZLANSKY: Anything. Any way you say it has to be; just say yes.

ZILINSKY: Do you think that I relish the prospect of living in exile? This deal will make the papers, it'll make me one of "those guys" you read about, criminals living on some beach—do you imagine that I wanted that for myself? Never to be able to walk down Madison Avenue again? I'm not an old man, and I'm giving all that up! Never to—you know— I at least feel somehow a *part* of American life. A small part but relevant to the whole thing. I mean—voting—

MIZLANSKY: *You* vote?

ZILINSKY: No, but I can if I want to! If someone actually came along! And if I wanted to, I could! There's patriotism: the pull of your country!

MIZLANSKY: What are you, Whittaker Chambers all of a sudden? It's a little business deal, not the pumpkin papers!

ZILINSKY: No! Being part of the discourse, part of the American dialogue, part of democracy! And all that will be taken from me. All these aspects you seem to take for granted! I don't know if you'll miss them, but I know I will! For what?

MIZLANSKY *(Trying not to laugh)*: No, I can see this is a serious issue with you. I had no idea you took your citizenship so seriously.

ZILINSKY: So the thing to do is figure out what it's worth to you. To have me sell my right to be part of the dialogue.

MIZLANSKY *(Amused)*: It's nice that your patriotism is so malleable, Sam. My God, don't fool yourself here that you're negotiating out of love of country; this is about not wanting to fly economy.

ZILINSKY: Call it what you want. If you want the deal, you have no choice—and that gives me a certain pleasure too, Davis. I want sixty percent of the De Vries deal.

MIZLANSKY *(Laughing)*: Sixty?

ZILINSKY: I swear to you, on the life of Sylvia Zilinsky and my children and my mother—if you try and negotiate with me on this, I will walk away and it's over. I'm not going to discuss it or bargain here, Davis. It's a one-time-only take-it-or-leave-it offer.

(Pause.)

MIZLANSKY *(Beat. Stiff)*: We aim to please. You've got yourself a deal.

(They shake hands.)

Congratulations, Sam. You're going to be rich. *Again.* For the last time in your life. Of course, the big trick for you will be not to blow it all on cute green shoes from Tokyo. *(Beat)* Personally, I give you about a year and a half.

(Lights down.)

SCENE 2

December 15. Lunchtime. Up on a booth at La Talpa, a dingy Mexican restaurant in West L.A. Tolkin and Hart. Mexican pop music wafts softly from the bar.

HART *(Eating)*: God, this is hot!

TOLKIN *(Also eating)*: Spicy place! That red sauce—!

HART: So, now, what it comes down to, reading between the ghastly lines of what my agents tell me, is that I'm unemployable *still*. Because of the last time I slipped. Two years ago. Two. Two years of meetings and chips and being straight—I get hired to play drunks—only these drunk guys!

TOLKIN: But you're still well known. People ask for your autograph—you get approached all the time! It's just you have to ride out the reputation you got as martinis-at-noon guy. When they saw you at the Beverly Hills Players drinking at eleven in the morning, before you did *Light up the Sky*—

HART: I hope I get this space thing. They've asked if I'm available to play the Skeen-atope ambassador, guest star, six episodes. So . . . who knows? Maybe something . . . *(He shrugs, casual)* Who knows, maybe it would lead to a regular thing.

TOLKIN: I'm sorry? A *what*? A Skeen-a-what?

HART: Tope. *Skeen-atope.* It's a kind of a space rodent on *Star Attack.* You've seen—the—you know—with the scrunchy face and the furry—but if you do it, then you can go to—they—they have these crazy weekend conventions and you can pocket fifteen grand—a Skeen-atope ambassador can easily pocket ten grand cash. At an Airport Hyatt.

TOLKIN: Really?

HART: Oh yes. You sign cards and autograph and—crazies all come out for it. *(Beat)* I tell you, the number-two special here, you don't have to eat all day; it's like *everything* at once! A burrito, a relleno, tacos, a chimichanga, a tostada, frijoles *and* tortillas! I love it here—the old L.A. It's so comfortable. You can have your Spago, your Trumps—your fancy—you can. *(Beat, with a mouth full of food)* Also! Also! The Taper—Gordon—they called! Maybe I'm going—maybe—Stoppard one acts—very frothy—very "ha, ha, ha!"

TOLKIN *(Interrupting)*: Listen, Lionel. I brought you to lunch because I've got good news for you.

HART: Really? Good news?

TOLKIN: There's a thing, a situation, maybe it could lead to us being able to do the Nazi picture, you know, if it works out right. *(Beat)* It's Mizlansky/Zilinsky.

HART: I see. Oh. Oh. Well. Mizlansky/Zilinsky. The schmucks. *(A sigh)* So, you got in with those guys, huh?

TOLKIN: No, don't say it like that. Just listen. I told you about their Bible thing. I'm—he gave me a terrific advance, and it seems a little kooky, but it's fast and—they need a guy to promote the product.

HART *(Contempt)*: They need a pitchman?

TOLKIN: They would like you to be the pitchman. You would meet the buyers, you would do a little promotional video. The star of *Tintoretto, Art Detective* . . .

HART: So it would be like a sideshow, I'd be the carny guy: "Step right up, step right up . . . Mizlansky/Zilinsky, the Bible! Leviticus! Step right up . . . !"

TOLKIN: Yes. Look. Fine. Have an attitude about it, but it's a chance at moving ahead a little bit. Out of the rut you're in. They're willing to pay you very well. Beyond very well.

HART: Well. I—I—all I have is my name. My good name. If this is illegal, if it's a Mizlansky/Zilinsky scam and my name is on it, I'm not gonna get called to do stuff . . .

TOLKIN: Like what, the space-rodent ambassador on *Star Attack*? Is that where your good name has—you know what—look, you know how certain books don't do well? They end up on that table—we're remaindered people. You're waiting for a call to play an intergalactic rodent! Come on here!

HART: That tone. I hate that tone. You sound like Mizlansky. You *sound* just like him. My friend: I am broke. But I can't risk what little I have. I can't be one of those guys. I was brought up to believe in . . . believe in myself, which is why I stopped drinking. I have my self-respect, but what I can't have is a best friend undermining me. What I can't have is a best friend who wants me dead.

TOLKIN: Let's not stand on ceremony here. Look. This might be a way to make the Nazi picture. You know, if you're so committed and passionate about making the Nazi picture,

I don't see how being the pitchman on this thing is so awful.

HART: No. I guess. I just . . .

TOLKIN: Is it any worse than—I mean, let's be honest. The Skeen-atope ambassador and an airport Hyatt? Is it that much more horrid for you?

HART: Well. I think it's—there's a certain dignity in—the Skeen-atope represents a—a—a quest for universal understanding and looking past—you know—physical appearances—

TOLKIN: Uh-huh. But you're saying there's dignity in going to the Hyatt and signing autographs as a space rat. Just so we're clear here.

HART: Please. Allow me to feel about this the way I need to feel, Alan. Okay? If I need to have *illusions*, then let me!

TOLKIN: Right. No. I understand that. I'm just trying to get you some money. What's so bad?

HART: I know. God. Can we just get the check? I had the extra guacamoles—you don't want to miss that, you know.

TOLKIN: So, will you come to the meeting? *(Beat)* Because it's good for the Nazi.

HART *(Highly agitated)*: I'll come. I don't want to—can we not talk about it? Right now, can we not? Please? Just tell me what I owe . . .

TOLKIN *(Taking out his wallet)*: It's fine. I'm taking you to lunch today, okay? Today, I've got it.

(Blackout.)

SCENE 3

5:15 P.M. The same day. Mizlansky's house. Mizlansky and Brook, wandering around in conference with Mr. Braithwait over the speakerphone. Braithwait is a man with a rural twang. Sam Zilinsky sits absolutely still, listening.

MIZLANSKY: Okay, I'm just trying to catch up with you, Mr. Braithwait, is all I'm saying here.

BRAITHWAIT *(Over speakerphone)*: That's fine. Very hard to get hold of you. I called your New York partner, Mr. Zilinsky, I had been his client, and I got no answer, so I hope you don't mind—

MIZLANSKY: I'm glad you had the good sense to call me here.

BRAITHWAIT *(Over speakerphone)*: See, the thing is, we bought three titles from you, through Lewis Peckmeyer, c.p.a., of Elbow Lake, Minnesota.

MIZLANSKY *(Trying not to laugh)*: He's a good man.

BRAITHWAIT *(Over speakerphone)*: Now, he's—I can't seem to get him either—I'm a little worried. Those three titles are *Psalms Set to Dulcimer.*

MIZLANSKY: Great!

BRAITHWAIT *(Over speakerphone)*: *Exodus for Preteens.*

MIZLANSKY: I love that one!

BRAITHWAIT *(Over speakerphone)*: And *Water into Wine, Fishes into Loaves.*

MIZLANSKY: Very good choices.

BRAITHWAIT *(Over speakerphone)*: But the problem is the Psalms thing has no dulcimer; there's no music at all, and the Exodus is really—well—sort of Deuteronomy, though I don't recall anyone named Shirley in the Bible . . . and the third—the fishes one—well—sir—that's just a blank.

MIZLANSKY: Are you kidding me? How could this happen?

BROOK: Mr. Braithwait. I'm Miles Brook, head of product standards here at Old Brompton Corporation, and what I think happened is that somehow some incomplete tapes were—in the mail room—it's nuts—were packed accidentally. *(Beat)* See, we had some . . . *(Beat. He sighs)* We had, as a part of a church program, hired some inner-city youths, some minority kids, and the truth is, the sad and hard fact is, they actually couldn't read—and were too shy to say, and so we had a bad, *bad* day before we figured that out, and all sorts of mishaps occurred.

(Pause. Mizlansky looks thrilled at this story. He shakes his head.)

MIZLANSKY: Yeah. See, *you* ended up with the mistakes! Now, these poor ghetto kids; it's a big problem, but it's a very vital part of our program. We have the backing of several—the Congressional Black Caucus! These kids! We're training them, slowly, but we feel obligated to go through it with the kids. At any rate, it will all be resolved by tomorrow. And it's great to meet you like this. Oh, what a pleasure! If you come to L.A. at all, we're in the book, we're located in . . .

(Beat. Brook gesticulates wildly.)

. . . right . . . near the airport. Merry Christmas and Happy New Year. Bye.

(Mizlansky hangs up and sighs.)

Okay. Now. We have Tolkin fix this; we let Trecker handle these things, Jesus, he's such an asshole! He's stealing from me, because he gets paid a bonus for every master recording—I can't do it all, man! I can't be in charge of—you know I'm holding it all—I'm having a—my hiatal hernia! It's like an acid milkshake!

TOLKIN *(Entering with Hart)*: Hello, Davis. I brought an old friend with me.

MIZLANSKY *(Spreads his arms to envelop Hart. Solemn)*: Lionel. Look at you. My God. It's been—it's been way too long, my friend. And you both remember Sam.

HART *(Shy)*: Oh, hi. Yeah. God. It's been, wow. I don't know. Maybe? What? A . . . million years . . . ?

ZILINSKY *(He turns to Hart with great affection)*: You look terrific, Lionel.

HART: So do you, Sam. I guess New York is good for you.

ZILINSKY: You know I heard you on the radio last year doing a Brecht play. I had to pull over and just listen, you know, on the Santa Monica Freeway.

HART: I know. I loved your note. It meant a lot to me.

(Pause.)

MIZLANSKY: And this is our attorney, the quick-witted and brave-hearted Miles Brook.

HART: Hi.

BROOK: I have to tell you. We go to the theatre a lot, my wife and daughter and I. We saw your *Endgame*. Staggering.

HART: My God! You saw that? In Pomona? At Teatro under Los Stars?

BROOK: We love Beckett, what can I say, it's nuts. Also did I read you're working with Mike Nichols on his new picture?

HART *(After a beat)*: Oh. No. People are always making this mistake. That's Heart. With an "e." No relation. He's never done theatre.

MIZLANSKY: Anyway—you look just great. Amazing to see you! Fit and—in a good place. And I know you've been through some turbulence. But it's the rough parts that make the good stuff matter, right? When did we do *Sidewinder Summer*?

HART: Oh, God, seventy-three? Seventy-four. I remember I had a maroon leather fringe hat.

MIZLANSKY: People still talk about you being eaten by the snakes. Six minutes of viper mastication. Close-ups. Wide-angles. Chewing. Leaping. Kicking.

ZILINSKY: The kid who directed that completely vanished. It was as if the experience had so utterly demoralized him that he—he went into the witness-protection program or something.

TOLKIN: I knew him, Burt Salks, he became a rolfer in Tel Aviv, cleaning up.

ZILINSKY: Smart kid. Got out quick.

HART: That was a rough shoot. In the desert, no food. Those snakes everywhere . . .

MIZLANSKY: We had some real great days, didn't we? Li, were you in the thing I did with the hippies? The orgy thing? *Patchouli Blowup* . . .

HART *(Laughing)*: In it? I had to be naked! I was finger painted by naked people! I had to close my eyes! Oi, I can still feel those hands! I took a shower and cried afterward! I had bottle-green water paint on my pee-pee!

(Pause. The room is silent. He extracts a script from his bag.)

But we've moved on to more adult pursuits, haven't we? This is the Nazi—

MIZLANSKY *(Cuts him off)*: Yes. That was a great period. The Golden Age! Of independent outfits. You could make a picture in a few days back then, and if it had the word "Harley" in the title, sell it to South America for a fortune!

HART: Yeah . . . And-and-and—you know—do good work too! Right?

(Pause.)

MIZLANSKY: Lionel. We're so thrilled that you're here with us. Has Alan showed you what we're doing with these recordings? It's very exciting.

HART: Sounds like a lot of fun. Children's Bible stories.

MIZLANSKY: Yeah, we're going to get you to narrate a little bit of Noah and the Ark.

HART: I've done a lot of kid's theatre, I really love doing it; I started out with The Trotsky Tots Company in Pittsburgh in '65. I played a Marxist sheep on a kibbutz—"Baaa—and together."

MIZLANSKY: Great! Wonderful! Look. Al—listen—I need to get you working on quality control on the masters—Paul will show you—

TRECKER *(Entering)*: Mr. De Vries is here. I put him by the pool. He wants to hear one of the Job series.

TOLKIN: Quality control?

TRECKER: Should I give him something, Davis? Sacher torte? Percodan? What?

MIZLANSKY: Don't make jokes, Paul. Okay? We have normal people present.

ZILINSKY *(To Trecker)*: Paul. See if there's a little Pellegrino and drop in a dash of bitters, would you?

(Trecker crosses to a small bar and gets him a drink.)

HART: Uh, Davis. I have the Nazi script. I know Al mentioned it.

MIZLANSKY: I hear there's real buzz on it.

HART: Well. We had a meeting with a group of retired rabbis who said they might be willing to help with financing.

MIZLANSKY: Maybe we should have a cocktail party for the rabbis. A serious roundtable discussion where we explore the—you know—issues. And we could serve a light meal. But I'd hate to give them script approval.

ZILINSKY *(Smiling)*: God forbid.

MIZLANSKY: You know what rabbis can be like.

BROOK: I think that's right. The many issues. We should explore. Before committing.

HART: And I . . . of course, you know, the part of Mort Mandleman, Nazi hunter, was written for me.

MIZLANSKY: It's the perfect marriage between an actor and a part, Lionel.

BROOK: If the Beckett fest was any indication; wonderful.

HART: Maybe we can marry the rabbis with De Vries's people.

MIZLANSKY: Miles. Alan. Take Lionel out to the pool, why don't you, and introduce him to Horton. Chat, we'll call you back in here in a few minutes.

(Tolkin and Hart exit. There is silence. Mizlansky glowers at Trecker.)

ZILINSKY: Thanks, Paul. Very good for a sour stomach. The bitters. Soothe.

TRECKER: Oh, really?

(Mizlansky snorts.)

TRECKER *(Defensive)*: What? Is something the matter?

MIZLANSKY *(Courtly)*: Nothing, Paul. Is there anything *I* can do for *you?*

TRECKER *(Nervous)*: Uhm. Davis. Should I play them the Job tapes? They're here . . . they're waiting.

MIZLANSKY *(Calm)*: And are the Job tapes, tell me, Paul, are they actually, oh, I don't know, *presentable?* To the public? Or is something missing? Like the *sound?*

TRECKER: Was there a problem? Is there something *wrong?* What? Whatever it is—I didn't do it!

MIZLANSKY: Hey, *you* know when you're being duplicitous. I trust you, man, and you're just ripping me off, just like all the rest. But that's fine, why you should be different— another lazy, shifty kid with a daddy problem, and I want my Rolex, which you stole from off my bedside table, and the ancient Egyptian ceramic cats you took from the library. Because this is not working out. I have too much other stuff to do to take time out to play daddy.

TRECKER *(Furious)*: Hey, I'm here twenty-four hours a day. Lying to creditors, making tapes, getting take-out mint kasha! As for the stupid Bible-story tapes: I've hired every out-of-work actor and writer and musician in this town who will actually perform for drug or booze money and who might be able to deliver something actually *audible. (Beat)* Plus I didn't take your crappy fake ceramic Metropolitan Museum gift-shop cats, as if I would! I didn't have time: I was too busy dodging IRS callers! And your stupid fake Rolex—*you gave me!* It cracked!

(Pause. Mizlansky smiles.)

MIZLANSKY: What can I say? "I am sorry." When you're right, you're right. Man, do I love you. *Man, do I respect you.* So deeply, more than my own misbegotten children, do I love you, a man who can stand up to me! Let me tell you: this business is almost over. And I'm going to take the people who have been loyal to me on a grand European tour: you two guys, Esther, that's it. Right now, I love you more than I have ever loved the *drek* that sprung from my loins. Right now, if I could, if I had an empire, I would give it to you.

(Beat. Trecker exits.)

ZILINSKY: So.
MIZLANSKY: So. Let's bring them in. Let's be clearheaded and close this.

(Blackout.)

SCENE 4

6:20 P.M. The same day. Mizlansky's living room. Dusk. Mizlansky, Zilinsky, Trecker, Brook, Tolkin, Hart and De Vries. They are listening to one of the Bible-story recordings. The narrator is Trecker, accompanied by a synthesizer.

TRECKER *(On tape):* . . . And his name was Job. And he was an honest, hardworking fellow. He never did wrong. He feared God, was loyal and good and shunned evil, and he prospered. He was very successful! With good children who loved him and were loyal! He had thousands upon thousands of camels, oxen and sheep—all of which made him a *very wealthy man*!

(The music swells to underscore the importance of this fact.)

MIZLANSKY *(Over the music)*: At Kmart there was a mob swarming over this. It was as if the Beach Boys were in the store.

TRECKER *(On tape)*: And he had hundreds of servants. His house was famous for the great Christmas parties—he was a famous man, he had everything a man could wish for. A loving and loyal wife, the envy of his fellow citizens . . . when he caught the eye of heaven!

(An ominous musical stirring.)

DE VRIES *(Over the music)*: It's very . . . dramatic. Don't you think, Lionel?

HART *(Hushed)*: It's great! It's *moving*.

DE VRIES: Could we have a drink?

MIZLANSKY: Paul. Let's all have a scotch.

BROOK: I wouldn't mind a Manhattan.

TRECKER *(Fierce)*: Quiet! This is the good part!

(Trecker pours scotch for all. Music swells.)

HART *(As Trecker hands him a scotch)*: No scotch for me, a water— a glass—

(He puts the glass down.)

TRECKER *(On tape)*: He was a holy man; you couldn't get any holier than Job. He'd offer burnt offerings on behalf of his children in case they'd offended God.

ZILINSKY *(Sotto voce)*: You're kidding me, right? This is an elaborate practical joke, right?

MIZLANSKY *(Quietly)*: Hey, you walked away. Someone had to be in charge of production.

TRECKER *(On tape)*: And God was so proud, he said to Satan, "See, see? There's nobody on Earth like my servant Job!" But Satan said, "Sure, he's God-fearing *now*, you've treated him well, it's easy for him, but take away his blessings, take away his possessions, he'd turn on you like *that*."

ZILINSKY *(Whispering, singsong, delighted)*: Oh, I think I know who wrote *this* one.

TRECKER *(On tape)*: "If you made life hard for him, he'd turn, because, God," sneered Snatan—*Satan*—"that's what people are like." But God laughed at this and said, "Satan: I accept the challenge."

(Dramatic music.)

MIZLANSKY: Why don't we finish our drinks and go down to Trader Vic's for a bite? I've heard enough. Lionel, are you hungry?

HART: Yeah, sure.

ZILINSKY *(Smiling)*: Well, let's just hear a little more. This is the best part of the story.

TRECKER *(On tape)*: "And then the fires of punishment rain down! The oxen are slaughtered en masse, and the donkeys stolen by marauding Arab thieves, the sheep are burnt to death as are the shepherds, and a tornado wipes out the kids. Job, reeling in anguish, never blames God! And God turns to Satan and says, "See—not a word of blasphemy out of my loyal servant Job!" And the devil says, "Oh yeah? Hurt him where it hurts and he'll betray you without batting an eye!" And God responds "Never!" And then Job is afflicted like never before; a miasma of sorrows strikes him without regard to his dignity or honor; endless pain, boils and ulcers . . . And his wife said, "You still refuse to blame God?" And Job responds as follows: "Foolish woman. You have to take the good with the bad."

(Zilinsky reaches over and turns off the tape player. There is a silence. Zilinsky laughs finally.)

ZILINSKY: Delightful, right?

MIZLANSKY: Yes! Terrific!

DE VRIES: Oh, yes. The moral tone! The way it so beautifully sets up the wrath and power of the Almighty!

MIZLANSKY: Yes, we were going for a sober, harsh . . . uh . . . feel.

ZILINSKY: Oh yeah. It's pretty clear what this thing is, isn't it, Horton, Davis?

DE VRIES: Has a kind of a . . . what . . . ? A homemade quality. Good old American homemade. *Hand*made. Yes!

ZILINSKY: Homemade things are the best things.

(Beat.)

DE VRIES: Yes. *(Beat)* Outside of Tulsa, we have an orchard. Granny Smith, McIntosh, Golden Delicious. The kids collect the apples. We make apple brown betty for our friends.

MIZLANSKY *(Nervous)*: God, do I love apple brown betty.

HART: Me too. I don't think anyone in L.A. makes it . . .

TOLKIN *(Smiling wildly)*: Oh, it's the best.

DE VRIES: I'll FedEx you some. My Farlette makes them herself.

ZILINSKY: Farlette?

DE VRIES: My daughter. *(Beat, sotto voce, a secret)* She uses nutmeg.

MIZLANSKY: But I think I understand. Your point is, "These are the things we work for." Right? This is what it's all about.

DE VRIES: Oh, yes. Exactly. Eh, Lionel?

HART *(Finally)*: It's very important to give children a foundation.

ZILINSKY: Of course, these tapes are not *unlike* apple brown betty, are they not? In many respects.

MIZLANSKY: Ah-hah. Yes! Right! Exactly!

ZILINSKY: Of course, apple brown betty has a longer shelf life.

(Pause.)

MIZLANSKY: Ha-ha-ha. Oh, Sam, so funny. Droll, droll, droll.

DE VRIES: I do so love a nice single malt in the early evening, it sure does help pave the way for the closing of a deal.

ZILINSKY *(Drinking)*: Yeah. It does. Doesn't it? *(Beat)* Cheers. To the closing of deals. *(Thoughtful pause)* I suppose drinking helps because it makes it easier, doesn't it? . . .

DE VRIES: Easier?

ZILINSKY: Yes . . . To screw and to be screwed.

(They clink glasses. De Vries shakes his head.)

MIZLANSKY *(Tilting his head; a threat)*: Not everyone is quite so ambivalent about business, Sam. To some people it's not sullying.

DE VRIES *(Drinking, laughing)*: No. He's right, Davis. The scotch. Yes. It helps smooth the discussion of moneys. You're not drinking, Lionel?

HART *(Self-conscious)*: I don't. I just watch, I'm sorry to say. Liquor and I are a bad match. For a long time we were a good match, but then one day it just . . . a bad marriage. We got divorced. *(Shrugs)* Was impossible for me. I couldn't quite act. I forgot how to perform. Without it. And then with it.

DE VRIES: I just have to say, I can't believe I'm sitting here with Lionel Hart.

HART *(Nervous)*: Here I am. In the flesh.

DE VRIES: Is there any chance they're going to be bringing back *Tintoretto*?

HART: Agh. There's—it was a show that was ahead of its time. It was a little too clever; too "in." Too hip.

DE VRIES: Maybe if you teamed up with Rockford.

TOLKIN *(A deep sigh, nostalgic)*: It was a great show. Politically it really was very out there.

MIZLANSKY: Sometimes the public isn't ready. It's happened to me, I think, with *Dune Buggy Chickadee*.

DE VRIES: So, Lionel, you're going to be out there, promoting the product?

HART *(Looking around)*: Yeah, I guess I am . . .

DE VRIES: Well. If you're involved, Lionel, it gives a certain class to the thing. *(Beat)* You know, my clients would be over the moon if we could get Lionel to Tulsa to do an evening, play some of the recordings . . . maybe do a monologue from *Tintoretto*.

HART: Oh. Go to Tulsa?

DE VRIES *(Patting Hart's leg)*: We have a nice country club, we put people up. Cowboy-motif bunkhouses. Give you a sirloin at the Oilman's Club, show you the oil wells. Shale, flames shoot up, very dramatic. Like something out of the Book of Revelation.

ZILINSKY: It's a rather magnificent part of the country, Lionel.

HART: Uh-huh. Tulsa. I've never been.

DE VRIES: *And* Enid, where we have a group of dentists who buy dozens of these things . . . they'd have a—take you out, hunt wild boar, grill it over a spit.

HART: Boar? Wild boar?

TOLKIN: I hear it's very special. The taste.

HART *(Weakly)*: We have some interesting movie projects in the works, Horton. The hunt for Nazis in America.

MIZLANSKY: Something we're developing for Lionel.

HART: Mort Mandleman, Nazi hunter. Based on his work.

DE VRIES: It's a complicated, interesting story, and one which tends to get told only from one very particular point of view.

HART: Excuse me?

DE VRIES: I would hope you were going to take a more balanced approach.

HART *(Grinning)*: Balanced? About Nazis hiding from justice? Are you—

DE VRIES: Look at it from the other side, maybe. *Balance.*

HART *(Not sure what he's hearing)*: Balance? Did you say *balance?*

ZILINSKY *(Over this)*: Balance. Yes. Balance.

MIZLANSKY *(Warning, over this)*: Oh, We'll be very evenhanded. We won't play sides. No. We'll present the truths. *(Beat)* Maybe we should get down to looking at some of the numbers; after all, if you're buying all these titles, we're going to need time to prepare them.

TOLKIN *(Gently prying Hart away)*: Perhaps we should get to our story conference in Burbank, Lionel.

HART: Oh, sure, yeah . . .

DE VRIES *(Slapping Hart's thigh)*: No, don't go, you'll miss the best part, see, these two fellows here, Lionel, they're going to try and Jew me out of my finder's fee.

(Mizlansky laughs. Zilinsky is stone-faced. Tolkin chuckles. Hart looks like a stone. The temperature in the room changes.)

HART: They're going to what? They're *what?*

DE VRIES *(A mock whisper and a twinkly laugh)*: Jew me out of my finder's fee.

(Silence.)

MIZLANSKY: Look. Let's just—before we discuss finder's fees: maybe Paul should bring us a little something. I just got a case of briny olives from a little grove in Umbria. They just burst when you pop them between your teeth . . .

BROOK: That sounds wonderful! Wonderful!

HART *(Shaking his head)*: You know, I have to tell you right here and now: I don't appreciate that kind of remark.

TOLKIN: Oh, come on now, Lionel, he was just kidding.

ZILINSKY: I think he sorta meant it.

(Silence.)

HART *(To Tolkin, an angry whisper)*: I didn't know this is what it was going to be!

DE VRIES *(Apologetic)*: Oh, now. I'm sorry. I didn't mean to give offense. It was a little joke. I'm friendly with several Jewish families back home in Tulsa. The Golds. The Silvers. Really. Forgive me. I just meant to say that I'm not buying unless I take ten percent back home in cash.

ZILINSKY: Yes. We understand that, Horton. You've made that clear, I think. You want to double-dip.

MIZLANSKY: Hey, you guys: come on.

HART *(Rising)*: Look. I don't care about kickbacks, I'm not comfortable being the shill for anti-Semites.

DE VRIES *(Moaning)*: Lionel. I feel *terrible.* Really. You're an important part of this deal. Now. Let's just move on so we can all get what we need—

MIZLANSKY: Yeah, let's keep our eye on the deal, please.

HART *(Shaking his head, embarrassed)*: Yeah. I'm sorry. It's fine. It's just me. *(Beat. Furious)* Oh fuck it. Why should I apologize to you? All I have is my name and with you people—it's—

TOLKIN *(Interrupting. Almost laughing)*: Lionel. I beg of you. Can we not have an actor scene right now, *please?*

HART *(Astonished)*: Wait, wait. Wait. You think this is an *"actor thing"*? You think I'm causing a scene? This stuff matters, Alan—it's—*what matters!* You look back at this stuff and—

TOLKIN *(Moaning)*: Come on. None of it is *real*, really. It's just . . . they're just doing their deal, Lionel . . .

MIZLANSKY *(Quietly to De Vries)*: It was an inappropriate remark.

DE VRIES *(Sharper to Hart)*: And we move on, it really won't happen again. Sit down.

(Pause. Hart, seething, stays standing.)

DE VRIES: I don't really care for the phrase "kickback." But I wanted it to be clear; I put a fair bit of work into these deals, and you make a nice buck out of them, and so it goes. So . . . *(Beat. He looks at Lionel)* Are you going to sit down?

HART *(Quietly)*: Alan. You know, if you want to be a part of this, that's fine. If you're so weak that for money you'll let them trash us. God. Man . . . there is so much I have to be ashamed of in my sorry life, I'm full, I can't fit anymore in.

(Beat. There is silence.)

TOLKIN: I just don't see it as . . . quite so . . .

HART *(Gently to Tolkin and infinitely sad)*: Quite so . . . You can stay?

DE VRIES *(A soothing laugh, but a slight pressure behind it)*: Once again, Lionel. Understand me. Really. I'm very sorry for making you uncomfortable. It wasn't my intention. Why don't you just sit down and accept my apologies. You know, we're offering you something quite wonderful. The opportunity to represent a quality product. *(Beat)* Now let's face facts, Lionel. There's nobody in this room who thinks that we're about to lose you to a better offer any time soon. Is there? *(There is silence. Then ice)* So sit down, son.

HART *(Exploding)*: Oh fuck you, man, go fuck yourself, okay, fuck you— *(He turns to Tolkin)* Alan—walk away, really.

(Hart is shaking, waiting for Tolkin to respond. He doesn't.)

ZILINSKY *(Quietly)*: It's okay, Lionel. You're right to leave. Go home. Take a shower. Forget about this.

MIZLANSKY: Hey, I'm *paying* you to—

ZILINSKY *(Very soothing)*: Davis. Not now. See. This is a real person. He's having something called a real reaction. Okay?

(He pats Hart's arm gently, starts to lead him out. Hart pulls away violently.)

HART: Don't touch me! Fuck you, Sam! You're the worst of them all. You actually had potential to *do* something. You were different. You were better than these guys. You didn't have to be like them—

(He exits. There is a moment. Tolkin stands frozen, blanched.)

ZILINSKY *(Softly)*: Go after him, Alan.

TOLKIN *(Remote)*: What? Go . . . What? Should I . . . What?

ZILINSKY *(Disgusted)*: Go after your friend, Alan. He's your friend. Don't just *stand* there!

TOLKIN *(Looking around)*: Oh my God.

(He exits.)

MIZLANSKY *(After a moment)*: Okay, Mr. De Vries, you've had your fun, you want to play ball now, you getting what you need here?

DE VRIES: I really didn't mean to hurt people's feelings. I did want to get back home tonight . . .

MIZLANSKY: Then let's close the deal.

ZILINSKY *(After a moment)*: Well. I don't know. Davis. First things first: let's have a little "come to Jesus" with our dear friend Horton here.

MIZLANSKY *(Uncertain)*: Okay.

(There is a moment of silence between Davis and Sam.)

ZILINSKY: Okay. *(To De Vries)* So you want a kickback?

DE VRIES: It's quite common, Sam. A finder's fee.

ZILINSKY: Well, Davis, I just have to let it be said that because Horton's a ghastly, ill-mannered sadistic little hobgoblin, I'm disinclined to be quite so . . . *pliable.* To be quite so very malleable. *Vershteist?*

(There is a silence.)

ZILINSKY: That's Yiddish for "understand," Horton. *(Beat)* Do *you* understand?

DE VRIES: Sam. I don't have to buy your product. There are other shelter promoters just waiting for my call. But I think my purchase of one hundred and sixty-nine titles— right here—right now—I have the cashier's checks made out to Old Brompton Corporation in my briefcase—I think a finder's fee is a reasonable expectation.

BROOK: Certainly some sort of reward is called for, yes—

ZILINSKY *(Reasonable and deliberate)*: Oh. You don't get it: not one cent. No. Why is today not like other days? Because today, my friend, we don't make deals with *treif*, which is Yiddish for "filth." Actually, for "*pigs.*"

DE VRIES: Pigs.

MIZLANSKY *(Quietly. Ashen)*: Sam is not feeling well, Horton. Sam . . . sweetie . . . *(Gently to Zilinsky)* Do you want to rest and let me finish up here?

ZILINSKY: No. No. You see. I want to finish up here. I want this ugly loveless little life we have concocted here to finish itself up . . . please . . .

MIZLANSKY *(Moaning)*: Do this when we're alone, please, my friend . . . Really. *(Beat)* You don't want to do this now.

ZILINSKY: I think I do.

DE VRIES: Gentlemen . . . perhaps I should leave you alone to—

MIZLANSKY: Let's close our deal, Horton. You think ten percent—and I—

ZILINSKY *(Interrupts. Intense and odd)*: You know what would be great, Davis? If you actually told Mr. De Vries to piss on me, and we let him, as a part of it. As part of the entire *gestalt* of the Mizlansky/Zilinsky experience. If I submitted to him and his humiliation. Would that be fun, Horton? Davis?

MIZLANSKY: Sam is playing a little game. It's a joke. Right? A joke?

DE VRIES *(Not laughing, but crinkling)*: It's funny.

ZILINSKY: I would never joke about making money. Making a buck? We all know what a hard, bitter fuck of a trick that is, isn't it, Horton?

DE VRIES: Oh, yes, we do indeed.

(Sam looks at Davis. Mizlansky is smiling slightly. He has his head cocked at an angle and nods, casual and at ease.)

ZILINSKY: Since we're all agreed on how hard it is to make money, I would like to say, we will not sell you this product unless you make a five-percent donation to the United Jewish Appeal. Or the Negro College Fund, if that works for you. Or, say, Trecker, what's a gay group?

MIZLANSKY *(Wanting to leave)*: Stop it, Sam. Come on, Horton, let's maybe go down to—

ZILINSKY: Answer me, Paul.

MIZLANSKY: Do not answer him, Paul. This is a test of loyalty. Leave it alone Paul.

(Pause.)

TRECKER: ACT UP?

ZILINSKY: ACT UP. So, Mr. De Vries. What do you say? Now you have a choice. The kikes, the niggers, or the fags. Personally I would go with ACT UP, but that's because according to my Jewish analyst who escaped the death camps, I'm a closet case.

(Pause.)

DE VRIES *(Rising, polite, pleasant, clear)*: Gentlemen. I wish you well in your endeavors. I'm sorry we were unable to come to an agreement here today.

(He exits.)

BROOK: Let me talk to him. Let me see what I can do.

(He exits. There is silence.)

ZILINSKY: And there you have it. Mister Horton De Vries. The modern American businessman, doing business, flying around the country, making deals, engaging in trade to help the financial climate and adding to the general well-being of the nation.

MIZLANSKY: Why? Sam.

ZILINSKY: Hey. I just did a classic Mizlansky. I let my hostility get in the way. See? Fun, isn't it? You never know where it's gonna take you. You could go anywhere! And in the middle of the Book of Job, where he was besieged by—what was that marvelous phrase . . . ? Oh, yes: "a miasma of sorrows." I looked over at you and thought, "Hmmm, let's see how this looks on *him.*"

MIZLANSKY: What? For revenge?

ZILINSKY: Well. You know. I guess poor Hart just got to me. Just got under my skin. My very thin skin. He broke my heart. Funny. I didn't know they could do that anymore.

(Beat.)

MIZLANSKY: You don't give a fuck about Hart, you spineless piece of shit. You're just weak, Sam. Any chance you get to take the coward's way out—every time you see a chance to be the victim, you go for it. Hey. If you wanted to kill yourself, my friend, you should have just had the grace to slit your own goddamned throat by yourself in your hotel room instead of dragging me and *my life* down with you. Now get out.

ZILINSKY: I'm free. I'm free. Thank God, I'm free.

MIZLANSKY *(Still and soft and scary)*: And so am I.

ZILINSKY: Exactly.

(Zilinsky exits.)

DUSTY *(Entering, she carries a boom-box tape player and a bag containing oils and towels)*: Hi, Davis.

MIZLANSKY: Dusty! Jesus, what are *you* doing here?

DUSTY: *Davis.* You didn't forget, did you?

TRECKER: I rescheduled her for now.

MIZLANSKY: Hey, Paul. What are you still doin' here?

TRECKER: Huh?

MIZLANSKY: You don't work for me anymore . . . Hey. Kid. The playhouse is closed. You quit a few minutes ago, when you took Sam's side.

TRECKER: Davis. I'm sorry. I—

MIZLANSKY: No, no, no. See, you can play a little game out there in the world, eating off my plate and stabbing me in the back, and it's all funny and it's all material for you, but you gotta know—it ain't free . . . Dusty sweetie, I have a lot to do right now. This is the busiest time. I can't just be stopping for a rubdown. *(Beat. He looks at Trecker)* Come on kid, get your faggoty ass out of my fucking house! And by the way, I haven't forgotten. You have my old Adler typewriter at your house. I'll send someone to pick it up.

TRECKER: It's what I write on.

MIZLANSKY: I want that typewriter, and I'll send detectives to get it.

(Trecker exits. Beat. Davis stares at Dusty.)

DUSTY: Wow. There's a lot of really bad energy in this room. It's just like this haze of dark clouds . . .

MIZLANSKY: A haze?

DUSTY: You don't look so great, Davis.

(Dusty puts a tape into her boom box.)

MIZLANSKY *(Defensively)*: Well I'm *fine*. Look, kiddo . . . *(Beat. He looks at his watch)* Maybe we can split it into two short sessions?

DUSTY: Yeah, fine. But I need to charge a little extra for the drive up the canyon, and the gas, and wear and tear on the car, and—

MIZLANSKY *(Furious)*: Okay, okay, God, Come on . . . Do we have to negotiate? Does everybody—hey, you're supposed to calm me *down*, not get me hopped-up here! We're standing here haggling over a—

(He stops himself. The New Age music wafting out of the tape player has a soothing effect. Bells and gamelan jingle and ring out.)

Great music.

DUSTY: It was recorded under a pyramid.

(The music continues softly through the rest of the scene.)

MIZLANSKY: Oh.

DUSTY: Why don't you get ready. I can see your aura is gummed up. It's got *drek* on the edges.

MIZLANSKY: Well it's been a hard, hard day.

DUSTY: Well it's your business. It's just an awful business. People get so wiggy in the whole movie world . . . I know this completely firsthand, because you know that movie *Foxes*? I was Jodie Foster's stand-in. For one day. But the girls were all just crazy and mean . . . and super-bitchy to each other, and it was just one day, but people were like trying to "get to Jodie" and really jealous of me, so there would be these scenes at the craft service area. *(Beat)* And I just walked away because the energy was just black, black, black. And I really liked Jodie for trying to get away, move east, go to college, like she was going to try and have a whole new life. But I guess all the bad energy just sort of followed her from the movie business to college. Because that whole thing when David Brinkley shot the president. All that bad karma from the set of *Foxes*—around Jodie. I just got out. I just said, "I can't do this man. I quit."

MIZLANSKY: So, you just walked away from the business. *(Beat)* You didn't fight. It would have been a big opportunity for you. There aren't a lot of chances like that. Huh. *(Beat)* See, I can't. I've got to return fire. My brakes. I don't know. They just don't work. I go downhill, I accelerate. I've gotta return fire. I wish I could do that whole "walking away" thing.

(She lights a joint and gives him a toke.)

DUSTY: You've had a lot of work done on this house since the last time I was here. Like the pool was empty, and there was a dead coyote, and there was all that yucky yellow glass . . .

MIZLANSKY *(Absently)*: Yeah, I put a lot of work into the place. *(Beat)* They keep saying there's gonna be a mud slide. But it hasn't happened.

(Lights out on Mizlansky and Dusty. Trecker appears in a tight spotlight on the otherwise dark stage. The New Age music underscores Trecker's monologue.)

TRECKER *(In the near dark)*: And God said: "Let there be darkness so all is not light." So he created the night. And there was evening, and there was morning. The greater light to govern the day, and the lesser light to govern the night. And God saw all that he had made, and it was very good.

You don't know it at the time, driving away from the scene of the crime, as fast as you can, but it might be, in retrospect, the time in your life when you had the most joy.

I wasn't there to stop Mizlansky from picking up the phone when Firnbach called, and I wasn't there to warn Sam, and I wasn't there for the next time they saw one another, but I heard about it, and I missed them.

(Lights very slowly fade down on Trecker during the above and up on Zilinsky, who is alone, as lights come up on the Farmer's Market.)

SCENE 5

January 9, 1985. 4:00 P.M. The Farmer's Market. The late-afternoon sunlight-suffused upstairs dining area. A table. Metal chairs. Zilinsky is seated, reading a book. There are Christmas decorations. Mizlansky enters with coffee and a brown paper bag filled with donuts. Zilinsky looks shabby, worn.

MIZLANSKY: Hello, Sam.

ZILINSKY *(Not looking at him)*: I never understood why you like the Farmer's Market so much. It's so charmless. Exhausted. I hate it here.

MIZLANSKY: Oh, it's the other L.A. Not ours, you know. These people here, just trying to get by. Shuffling between the chow mein and the newsstand, the tourists. *(Pause)* Want a glazed raised?

(He holds out the bag. Zilinsky shakes his head.)

ZILINSKY *(Stiff)*: No. Nothing. Not from you. You have two minutes, that's it.

MIZLANSKY *(Sitting down)*: Relax, don't look so taut. It's not so bad, from what I hear.

ZILINSKY: It's not so *bad*, from what *you* hear? What, you have connections in the prisons? I'm sure you do, actually. But. No. No smiling here. Don't make light of this, Davis. I could die in there.

MIZLANSKY: I promise you, Sam, you will not die at the minimum-security facility in Danbury, Connecticut. It's like going to Pritikin on the low-sodium diet, at worst.

(Zilinsky does not smile.)

ZILINSKY: A few months. Is all it takes to kill you, Davis. A few months of concrete and misery.

MIZLANSKY: Oh come on. You give in too easily, Sam. That quality. Seriously: it won't be useful in there.

ZILINSKY: What an astonishing, cynical little man you are, Davis. Knowing everything you know before you know it. God. I always underestimate you. How far you'll go. Of course, I should have known, you made yourself a deal. On my back! On my back!

MIZLANSKY *(Shrugs, sighing)*: Reciprocity. It's a very tiring way to live. But still. I do believe in it.

ZILINSKY: You should have seen the feds when they came into my room at the Casa de la Ventana del Sol and took the money. You would have loved that. Sylvia there, crying. It was the high point of my adult life. Handcuffs and the smell of ammonia . . . you can't imagine.

MIZLANSKY *(Smiling)*: What can I say? I had no choice. I had to give them *something*.

ZILINSKY: Not something: you had to give them me. Never forget that. I'm—I'm curious. Since we're here. And will never speak again. Tell me: what are you going to do?

MIZLANSKY: Me, I don't know. Nothing great. I see Esther. I wander around town, killing time. I have this thing, I have to do fifteen million hours of community service at a daycare center in Watts. I like it. I like the kids. They're funny.

(He gets up.)

I want you to know: I . . . apologize.

ZILINSKY: Oh, no. You don't actually have that option. Not in this lifetime. It is irrelevant. And I didn't hear it. Look at me, Davis. I do not feel sorry for myself. There's just nothing left. I don't know what to do when I get out . . . What am I going to do?

MIZLANSKY: You'll figure it out. Christ, Sam, I'm sorry but it's your choice: give up or not. You know—there are only two plots in this life: the one that works out the way it should, and the one that doesn't.

ZILINSKY: God. I hate the way in California the Christmas decorations stay up into *February*. It's such bad *form*. In New York, you know, people move on, they're down by December twenty-sixth practically.

MIZLANSKY: I like it. I wish they'd stay up all year. Christmas in July. Anyway . . . I've got to go. I stole Esther's car. I've got to get it back to her.

ZILINSKY: I used to have one goal: I just wanted to be at peace with you. Not love you or hate you. Just to be at peace. Stupid. A pacifist's mistake. I really should have gone to war with you. If only I could have motivated myself to do that. God. What I could have done to you. The carnage. The damage. The havoc I could have inflicted. I have such instincts for the jugular. And I tamp them down. I never let them show. Entire municipalities burn and fall in my head. And such a mistake to pretend to be civilized when the world is only made whole by people like *you*. Killing and devouring. Going into battle.

MIZLANSKY *(Shrugs)*: Hey. Go to town. If hating me helps you get through the day, so go hate.

(He starts to exit.)

ZILINSKY *(Picking up the paper bag)*: You left your donuts.

MIZLANSKY: Yeah.

ZILINSKY *(Staring at him)*: Heavy donuts, Davis.

(Zilinsky holds out the bag, weighing it.)

MIZLANSKY *(Shrugs)*: For you. For after Danbury. *(Beat)* You know that thing I do? Hiding stuff from myself? Because I'm afraid someone will steal it?

ZILINSKY *(He looks inside. He takes out a ceramic sculpture of a cat)*: It's a clay cat? *(Beat)* The Egyptian?

MIZLANSKY *(Sighing)*: You know I have two, right? I thought I had hidden them in the attic. From *myself*. But the kid came by. He had them. He *had* taken them.

ZILINSKY: You trained him well.

MIZLANSKY *(Smiles)*: Anyway. If you want. Think about it: there's a buyer. This guy wants to buy them. Only as a pair. Keeps calling. The number's in there. A Mister Hamzer in Laguna Beach. Driving me crazy. *(Beat)* But . . . cash. If we sold 'em together . . . I mean, I don't know . . . you know . . . *(Beat)* A cushion.

ZILINSKY: A cushion, huh?

(He looks at the cat.)

Huh. I'm not at all sure I want to sell it.

MIZLANSKY: Oh.

ZILINSKY: I always liked this cat. I might want to *keep* it. To just look at it.

MIZLANSKY *(Casual)*: Well, you let me know. If you want to make the deal . . . It's the pair or nothing at all.

ZILINSKY *(Quietly, looking at the cat)*: Right. Only sold as a pair. *(Beat)* Like socks.

MIZLANSKY *(Leans down and kisses the top of Sam's head gently)*: You'll be okay, Sam.

ZILINSKY: Davis. Remember that first day. Sixty-six. We had that little office on Beverly. I was sitting there alone. We had

our first picture. Our first deal. And you ran in, and you
said, "They signed, they signed. It's our town . . ."

MIZLANSKY *(Lost)*: It's our town . . .

*(The two men stare at each other. Zilinsky gently, absently pets the
ancient ceramic cat.)*

END OF PLAY